Math Like a NINJA

ANDREW JENNINGS

BLOOMSBURY EDUCATION

LONDON   OXFORD   NEW YORK   NEW DELHI   SYDNEY

BLOOMSBURY EDUCATION
Bloomsbury Publishing Plc
50 Bedford Square, London, WC1B 3DP, UK
29 Earlsfort Terrace, Dublin 2, Ireland
BLOOMSBURY, BLOOMSBURY EDUCATION and the Diana logo are trademarks of Bloomsbury Publishing Plc
First published in Great Britain 2023 by Bloomsbury Publishing Plc
This edition published in Great Britain 2023 by Bloomsbury Publishing Plc

A catalogue record for this book is available from the British Library.

ISBN: PB: 978-1-8019-9196-4; ePDF: 978-1-8019-9195-7; ePub: 978-1-8019-9197-1

2 4 6 8 10 9 7 5 3 1

Text design by Jeni Child

Printed and bound in the UK by CPI Group Ltd, Croydon CR0 4YY

MIX
Paper | Supporting
responsible forestry
FSC
www.fsc.org FSC® C013604

To find out more about our authors and books visit www.bloomsbury.com
and sign up for our newsletters.

With thanks to Sarah Farrell and Paul Tucker for their expert advice and input.

Contents

Contents continued...

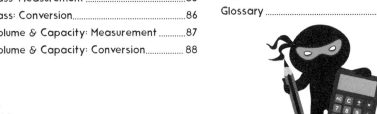

1 Number & Place Value

Numerals & Words to 10, 20, 100 & 1,000,000

To 20 in Ones

0 – zero	11 – eleven
1 – one	12 – twelve
2 – two	13 – thirteen
3 – three	14 – fourteen
4 – four	15 – fifteen
5 – five	16 – sixteen
6 – six	17 – seventeen
7 – seven	18 – eighteen
8 – eight	19 – nineteen
9 – nine	20 – twenty
10 – ten	

To 100 in Tens

10 – ten
20 – twenty
30 – thirty
40 – forty
50 – fifty
60 – sixty
70 – seventy
80 – eighty
90 – ninety
100 – one hundred

To 1,000,000

10 – ten	10,000 – ten thousand
100 – one hundred	100,000 – one hundred thousand
1,000 – one thousand	1,000,000 – one million

Hundred Square

Here are all the numbers to 100.

1	2	3	4	5	6	7	8	9	10
11	12	13	14	15	16	17	18	19	20
21	22	23	24	25	26	27	28	29	30
31	32	33	34	35	36	37	38	39	40
41	42	43	44	45	46	47	48	49	50
51	52	53	54	55	56	57	58	59	60
61	62	63	64	65	66	67	68	69	70
71	72	73	74	75	76	77	78	79	80
81	82	83	84	85	86	87	88	89	90
91	92	93	94	95	96	97	98	99	100

NINJA TIP:

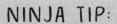
Moving down 1 space adds 10
Moving up 1 space subtracts 10
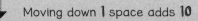
Moving right 1 space adds 1
Moving left 1 space subtracts 1

Number Lines

Number line from 0-10, counting in ones

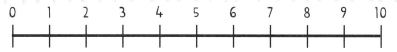

0   1   2   3   4   5   6   7   8   9   10

Number line from 0-20, counting in twos

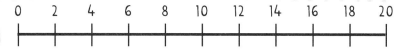

0   2   4   6   8   10   12   14   16   18   20

Number line from 0-30, counting in threes

0   3   6   9   12   15   18   21   24   27   30

Number line from 0-40, counting in fours

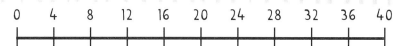

0   4   8   12   16   20   24   28   32   36   40

Number line from 0-50, counting in fives

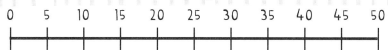

0   5   10   15   20   25   30   35   40   45   50

Number line from 0-60, counting in sixes

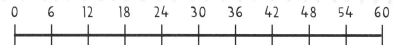

0   6   12   18   24   30   36   42   48   54   60

Number Lines (continued)

Number line from 0–70, counting in sevens

| 0 | 7 | 14 | 21 | 28 | 35 | 42 | 49 | 56 | 63 | 70 |

Number line from 0–80, counting in eights

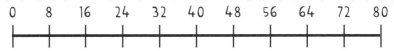

| 0 | 8 | 16 | 24 | 32 | 40 | 48 | 56 | 64 | 72 | 80 |

Number line from 0–90, counting in nines

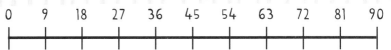

| 0 | 9 | 18 | 27 | 36 | 45 | 54 | 63 | 72 | 81 | 90 |

Number line from 0–100, counting in tens

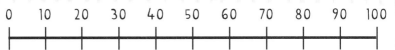

| 0 | 10 | 20 | 30 | 40 | 50 | 60 | 70 | 80 | 90 | 100 |

Number line from 0–110, counting in elevens

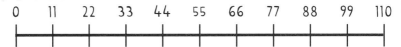

| 0 | 11 | 22 | 33 | 44 | 55 | 66 | 77 | 88 | 99 | 110 |

Number line from 0–120, counting in twelves

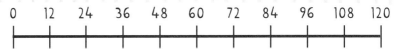

| 0 | 12 | 24 | 36 | 48 | 60 | 72 | 84 | 96 | 108 | 120 |

Negative & Decimal Number Lines

Number line counting in ones either side of 0

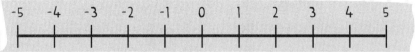

Number line counting in twos either side of 0

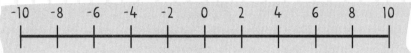

Number line counting in fives either side of 0

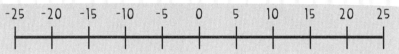

Number line counting in tens either side of 0

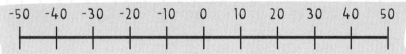

Number line counting in twenties either side of 0

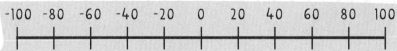

Decimal number line 0-1, counting in tenths

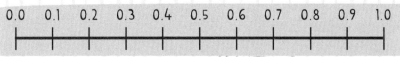

Place Value Grid

Place value grids help us understand how numbers become 10, 100 or 1,000 times bigger or smaller.

Ten thousands	Thousands	Hundreds	Tens	Ones
T Th	Th	H	T	O
2 (= 20,000)	2 (= 2,000)	2 (= 200)	2 (= 20)	2 (= 2)
4 (= 40,000)	6 (= 6,000)	3 (= 300)	1 (= 10)	5 (= 5)
9 (= 90,000)	7 (= 7,000)	8 (= 800)	8 (= 80)	2 (= 2)

NINJA TIP:

Each time a digit moves one column to the left, it becomes 10 times bigger. This involves multiplication (x).

Decimal	Tenths	Hundredths	Thousandths	In Full
.	t	h	th	
.	2 (= 0.2)	2 (= 0.02)	2 (= 0.002)	22,222.222
.	2 (= 0.2)	9 (= 0.09)	1 (= 0.001)	46,315.291
.	4 (= 0.4)	3 (= 0.03)	7 (= 0.007)	97,882.437

NINJA TIP:

Each time a digit moves one
column to the right, it becomes
10 times smaller.
This involves division (÷).

Greater Than 〉
Smaller Than 〈
Equals =

These symbols allow us to compare numbers.
The symbols allow us to show:
• which number is larger
• which number is smaller
• or if the numbers are equal in value.

〉   =   〈

greater than   equals   less than

NINJA TIP:

Remember that the side with the largest gap
points to the side with the largest number.

= means they're the same value. Simple!

Examples:

4 〈 7   3 〈 12   6 = 6   14 〉 7

Rounding

When rounding, you will often be asked to round the number to the nearest 10, 100, 1,000 or 10,000.

Step 1

Circle the place value you have been asked to round to.

to nearest 10	to nearest 100	to nearest 1,000
2,6(5)2	2,(6)52	(2),652

Step 2

Underline the digit to the right of the circled digit.

to nearest 10	to nearest 100	to nearest 1,000
2,6(5)2	2,(6)52	(2),652

Step 3

If the underlined digit is 4 or less, the circled digit stays the same.
If the underlined digit is 5 or more, the circled digit adds 1 more.

to nearest 10	to nearest 100	to nearest 1,000
2,6(5)2	2,(7)52	(3),652

Step 4

Change the digits to the right of the circled digit to zero.

to nearest 10	to nearest 100	to nearest 1,000
2,6(5)0	2,(7)00	(3),000

Estimating

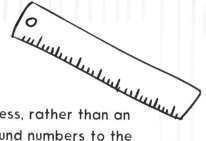

Estimating means to provide a best guess, rather than an exact answer. To estimate, we often round numbers to the nearest 10, 100 or 1,000 as they are easier to calculate.

Rounding to the nearest 10

exact	estimate
2 4 2	2 4 0
+ 2 6	+ 3 0
2 6 8	2 7 0

Rounding to the nearest 100

exact	estimate
5 8 7	6 0 0
- 2 3 1	- 2 0 0
3 5 6	4 0 0

NINJA TIP:

Estimating happens all the time in the real world.

Example: If we buy two items, one costing £4.67 (estimate / round to £5) and the other costing £9.79 (estimate / round to £10), we can quickly estimate that we will spend around £15.

Roman Numerals

Roman numerals are a different way of writing numbers.

1	I	11	XI	50	L
2	II	12	XII	100	C
3	III	13	XIII	500	D
4	IV	14	XIV	1,000	M
5	V	15	XV		
6	VI	16	XVI		
7	VII	17	XVII		
8	VIII	18	XVIII		
9	IX	19	XIX		
10	X	20	XX		

If a smaller number is after a bigger number, add it to the bigger number. Example: VI   V = 5 I = 1   5 + 1 = 6   VI = 6

If a smaller number is before a bigger number, subtract it from the bigger number. Example: IV   5 − 1 = 4   IV = 4

Ninja Maths Fact
Roman numerals are often used to represent years. MMXXII is 2022.

Ninja Maths Fact
Roman numerals are often used on clocks and on watches, so they might come up in questions on time.

Multiples

A multiple of a number is what you get when you multiply that number by an integer (whole number). In other words, a multiple of a number is when you count on in that number each time, e.g. 5, 10, 15, 20... The result is called the product. A multiple is essentially that number's times table.

x	1	2	3	4	5	6	7	8	9	10	11	12
1	1	2	3	4	5	6	7	8	9	10	11	12
2	2	4	6	8	10	12	14	16	18	20	22	24
3	3	6	9	12	15	18	21	24	27	30	33	36
4	4	8	12	16	20	24	28	32	36	40	44	48
5	5	10	15	20	25	30	35	40	45	50	55	60
6	6	12	18	24	30	36	42	48	54	60	66	72
7	7	14	21	28	35	42	49	56	63	70	77	84
8	8	16	24	32	40	48	56	64	72	80	88	96
9	9	18	27	36	45	54	63	72	81	90	99	108
10	10	20	30	40	50	60	70	80	90	100	110	120
11	11	22	33	44	55	66	77	88	99	110	121	132
12	12	24	36	48	60	72	84	96	108	120	132	144

Factors

A factor is a number that divides into another number without a remainder.

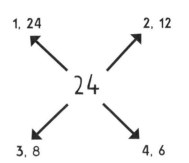

1, 24   2, 12

24

3, 8   4, 6

When finding factors, it helps to go through them in order: try 1 x, then 2 x, then 3 x, and so on.

NINJA TIP:

When finding factors, they come in pairs. When you divide the target number by one factor, the answer is another factor. Example:. 24 ÷ 12 = 2. 12 and 2 are a pair of factors.

Square numbers are a pair of the same number, e.g. 36 ÷ 6 = 6, but you only list the number once.

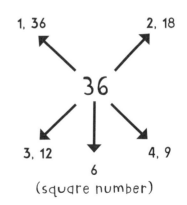

1, 36   2, 18

36

3, 12   4, 9

6
(square number)

Prime Numbers

Prime numbers are only divisible by one and themselves.
They only have two factors, called **prime factors**.
Composite numbers have more than two factors.

1	2	3	4	5	6	7	8	9	10
11	12	13	14	15	16	17	18	19	20
21	22	23	24	25	26	27	28	29	30
31	32	33	34	35	36	37	38	39	40
41	42	43	44	45	46	47	48	49	50
51	52	53	54	55	56	57	58	59	60
61	62	63	64	65	66	67	68	69	70
71	72	73	74	75	76	77	78	79	80
81	82	83	84	85	86	87	88	89	90
91	92	93	94	95	96	97	98	99	100

Examples: 7 only has two factors — itself and 1. It is prime.
14 has four factors — 1, 2, 7 and 14. It is composite.

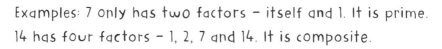

NINJA TIP:

Other than the number 2, all other even numbers can't be prime numbers because they can be divided by 2. That means they have at least three factors — 1, themselves and 2.

Square & Cube Numbers

A **square number** is a number that is multiplied by itself. For example, 4^2 means 4 x 4.

1^2 = 1 x 1 = 1

5^2 = 5 x 5 = 25

9^2 = 9 x 9 = 81

2^2 = 2 x 2 = 4

6^2 = 6 x 6 = 36

10^2 = 10 x 10 = 100

3^2 = 3 x 3 = 9

7^2 = 7 x 7 = 49

11^2 = 11 x 11 = 121

4^2 = 4 x 4 = 16

8^2 = 8 x 8 = 64

12^2 = 12 x 12 = 144

A **cube number** is a number that is multiplied by itself two times. For example, 4^3 means 4 x 4 x 4.

1^3 = 1 x 1 x 1 = 1

7^3 = 7 x 7 x 7 = 343

2^3 = 2 x 2 x 2 = 8

8^3 = 8 x 8 x 8 = 512

3^3 = 3 x 3 x 3 = 27

9^3 = 9 x 9 x 9 = 729

4^3 = 4 x 4 x 4 = 64

10^3 = 10 x 10 x 10 = 1,000

5^3 = 5 x 5 x 5 = 125

11^3 = 11 x 11 x 11 = 1,331

6^3 = 6 x 6 x 6 = 216

12^3 = 12 x 12 x 12 = 1,728

BODMAS / BIDMAS

BODMAS and BIDMAS are acronyms to help us remember the correct order to carry out calculation operations. Operations are actions, such as add or subtract.

B	O	D	M	A	S
Brackets	Order	Divide	Multiply	Add	Subtract
( )	$\sqrt{x}$ or x^2	÷	×	+	−

B	I	D	M	A	S
Brackets	Indices	Divide	Multiply	Add	Subtract
( )	$\sqrt{x}$ or x^2	÷	×	+	−

Ninja Maths Fact

BODMAS / BIDMAS moves from left to right. ÷ & × are equal in order. If they are both in a question, do them in the order written in the question. It's the same for + & −.

Try rewriting calculations until you only have two numbers and one operation remaining.

Example: $2^2 + 4 \times 3 = ?$

$4 + 4 \times 3 = ?$

$4 + 12 = 16$

Addition & Subtraction

Addition & Subtraction Vocabulary

ADDITION: +

plus	combine	increased by
add	altogether	more than
sum		

Parts of Addition

$$2 + 3 = 5$$

addend   operator   addend   sum or total

SUBTRACTION: −

minus	deduct	difference between
subtract	fewer than	decrease
take away	less than	

Parts of Subtraction

$$5 - 1 = 4$$

minuend   operator   subtrahend   difference

21

Addition & Subtraction Bonds

3 → 2, 1

2 + 1 = 3
1 + 2 = 3
3 - 1 = 2
3 - 2 = 1

4 → 1, 3

1 + 3 = 4
3 + 1 = 4
4 - 1 = 3
4 - 3 = 1

5 → 2, 3

2 + 3 = 5
3 + 2 = 5
5 - 2 = 3
5 - 3 = 2

6 → 2, 4

2 + 4 = 6
4 + 2 = 6
6 - 2 = 4
6 - 4 = 2

7 → 4, 3

4 + 3 = 7
3 + 4 = 7
7 - 3 = 4
7 - 4 = 3

8 → 5, 3

5 + 3 = 8
3 + 5 = 8
8 - 3 = 5
8 - 5 = 3

9 → 7, 2

7 + 2 = 9
2 + 7 = 9
9 - 2 = 7
9 - 7 = 2

9 → 5, 4

5 + 4 = 9
4 + 5 = 9
9 - 4 = 5
9 - 5 = 4

10 → 7, 3

7 + 3 = 10
3 + 7 = 10
10 - 7 = 3
10 - 3 = 7

Number bonds are pairs of numbers
that add up to make another number.

12
7   5

$7 + 5 = 12$
$5 + 7 = 12$
$12 - 7 = 5$
$12 - 5 = 7$

13
7   6

$7 + 6 = 13$
$6 + 7 = 13$
$13 - 6 = 7$
$13 - 7 = 6$

14
9   5

$9 + 5 = 14$
$5 + 9 = 14$
$14 - 5 = 9$
$14 - 9 = 5$

15
7   8

$7 + 8 = 15$
$8 + 7 = 15$
$15 - 7 = 8$
$15 - 8 = 7$

16
12   4

$12 + 4 = 16$
$4 + 12 = 16$
$16 - 12 = 4$
$16 - 4 = 12$

17
9   8

$9 + 8 = 17$
$8 + 9 = 17$
$17 - 9 = 8$
$17 - 8 = 9$

18
13   5

$13 + 5 = 18$
$5 + 13 = 18$
$18 - 5 = 13$
$18 - 13 = 5$

19
11   8

$11 + 8 = 19$
$8 + 11 = 19$
$19 - 11 = 8$
$19 - 8 = 11$

20
13   7

$13 + 7 = 20$
$7 + 13 = 20$
$20 - 7 = 13$
$20 - 13 = 7$

Number Bonds to 10: Tens Frame

0 + 10 = 10

1 + 9 = 10

2 + 8 = 10

3 + 7 = 10

4 + 6 = 10

6 + 4 = 10

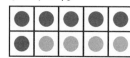

7 + 3 = 10

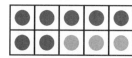

8 + 2 = 10

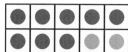

9 + 1 = 10

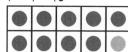

10 + 0 = 10

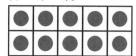

5 + 5 = 10

Addition Strategy:
Number Line & Partitioning

Partitioning is splitting a number into smaller parts to make it easier to work with.

Step 1

Draw a number line and place 0 at the beginning.

0

Step 2

Add the first number of the problem. Example: **32 + 14 = ?**

+ 32

0   32

Step 3

Partition the second number into smaller amounts which are easier to add. Add the separate parts one at a time.

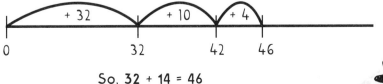

+ 32   + 10   + 4

0   32   42   46

So, 32 + 14 = 46

Addition Strategy: Partition & Jot

Partition and jot involves using your understanding of place value to separate numbers. In the example you can see we have separated – partitioned – the values of each number and jotted them down.

By separating the numbers into tens and ones, it is easier to do the sum by adding the tens together and adding the ones together, then adding them back together.

Examples:

```
  T O     T O
 (2)6  +  (3)2
  ↓  ↓    ↓   ↓
 20   6  30   2
```

Tens (T) = 20 + 30 = 50

Ones (O) = 6 + 2 = 8

50 + 8 = 58

```
  T O     T O
 (4)5  +  (3)6
  ↓  ↓    ↓   ↓
 40   5  30   6
```

Tens (T) = 40 + 30 = 70

Ones (O) = 5 + 6 = 11

70 + 11 = 81

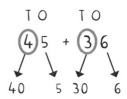

Addition Strategy: Column Addition

Column addition will help you add larger numbers together.

Step 1
Add the ones column, write the answer below.

```
  T O
  3 4
+ 2 5
-----
    9
```

Step 2
Add the tens column, write the answer below.

```
  T O
  3 4
+ 2 5
-----
  5 9
```

If the ones add up to 10 or more, the number will have tens and ones in it. If this happens, write the ones in the answer and 'carry' the tens into the tens answer by writing them under the line. Add the tens column, then add the extra tens.

Step 1
Add the ones column, write the answer below.

```
  T O
  4 7
+ 2 9
-----
    6
    1
```

Step 2
Add the tens column, then add the carried value to your answer. Write the total below.

```
  T O
  4 7
+ 2 9
-----
  7 6
    1
```

tens carried over ⟶

Addition Strategy:
Expanded Form & 3-digit Numbers

Expanded form helps us visualise hundreds, tens and ones vertically. This works for 4- and 5-digit numbers too.

Step 1   Add the ones, write the answer (8) below.

Step 2   Add the tens, write the answer (70) below.

Step 3   Add the hundreds, write the answer (100) below.

Step 4   Add the ones, tens and hundreds to get the total.

```
          1  4  2
       +     3  6
       _____
Step 1          8
Step 2       7  0
Step 3    1  0  0
       _____
Step 4    1  7  8
```

NINJA TIP:

See page 27 for more on what to do if the ones add up to 10 or more, or the tens to 100 or more.

Compact addition is the same process as expanded form, but you don't write out all the steps.

Step 1   Add the ones, write the answer in the answer row.

Step 2   Add the tens, write the answer in the answer row.

Step 3   Add the hundreds, write the answer in the answer row.

```
Step 1     1  4  2
Step 2  +     3  6
        _____
Step 3     1  7  8
```

Decimal Addition

first!

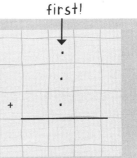

NINJA TIP:

The key to decimal addition is to create accurate place value. To do this, write your decimal points in first. Remember, they need to be placed in the same column. Now you can accurately place the numbers around the decimals.

NINJA TIP:

Try to give the decimal points their own square, right in the middle. Not on a line.

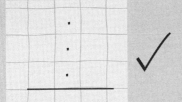

Examples:

43.6 + 29.4 = ?

```
   4 3 . 6
 + 2 9 . 4
 ─────────
   7 3 . 0
   1 1
```

56.4 + 3.27 = ?

```
   5 6 . 4
 +  3 . 2 7
 ──────────
   5 9 . 6 7
```

Subtraction Strategy: Number Lines & Counting Back

Step 1

Write the number you are subtracting from (minuend) on the right-hand side of the number line.
Example: 30 - 9 = ?

0   30

Step 2

Split the number you are subtracting (subtrahend) into chunks which feel easy to subtract. For example, instead of subtracting 9 from 30, subtract 5, then subtract 4.

0   21   25   30

So 30 − 9 = 21

NINJA TIP:

Counting back from tens is easy to do, so always try to do this first if possible. For example, if counting back 9 from 23, count back 3 to get to 20, then count back from 20 a further 6 to get to 14.

Subtraction Strategy: Counting Back with 3-digit Numbers

Step 1

Write the number you are subtracting from (minuend) on the right-hand side of the number line.

Example: 146 − 28 = ?

0   146

Step 2

Split the number you are subtracting (subtrahend) into chunks which feel easy to subtract. For example, instead of subtracting 28 from 146, subtract 10, then 10, then 6, then 2.

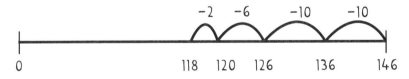

So 146 − 28 = 118

NINJA TIP:

Counting back in multiples of tens and hundreds is easy to do, so always try to do this if possible. For example, if counting back 90 from 230, count back 30 to get to 200, then count back from 200 a further 60 to get to 140.

Subtraction Strategy: Number Lines & Counting On

Your number line is now vertical. We are using counting on.

Step 1
Start with the number you're subtracting (subtrahend). This is now your starting point.
Example: 619 - 84 = ?

Step 2
Count on in sensible chunks / jumps to the number you are subtracting from (minuend).

Step 3
Add up the chunks / jumps you have taken to find the difference. This is your answer.

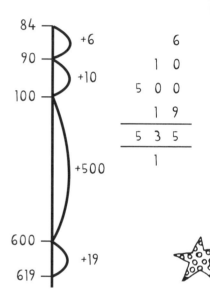

```
84 ┐
   │  +6          6
90 ┤              1 0
   │  +10     5   0 0
100┤              1 9
   │           ─────────
   │           5   3 5
   │  +500         1
   │
600┤
   │  +19
619┘
```

619 − 84 = 535

NINJA TIP:
Use easy chunks to count with, such as tens and hundreds.

Subtraction Strategy: Decomposition/Column Subtraction

Method with no exchange

Step 1
Write out the question with the larger number on top.

43 − 11 = ?

```
  4 3
 -1 1
 ─────
```

259 − 108 = ?

```
  2 5 9
 -1 0 8
 ───────
```

Step 2
Start in the furthest right column. Subtract the bottom number from the top. Write the answer (difference) below.

```
  4 3
 -1 1
 ─────
    2
```

```
  2 5 9
 -1 0 8
 ───────
      1
```

Step 3
Now move to the tens column and repeat. And again for the hundreds if there is one.

```
  4 3
 -1 1
 ─────
  3 2
```

```
  2 5 9
 -1 0 8
 ───────
  1 5 1
```

Subtraction Strategy Decomposition/Column Subtraction

Method with exchange

Within some subtraction questions, you need to take a larger digit away from a smaller digit, for example, 5 – 8.

When this happens, we have to borrow or exchange a digit from the column to the left. This is called **regrouping**.

Step 1 Write out the question.

Example 1: 45 – 38 = ?

```
    4 5
  - 3 8
  _____

  _____
```

Example 2: 274 – 35 = ?

```
    2 7 4
  -   3 5
  _____

  _____
```

Step 2 Start in the column with the smallest place value. If the top digit is smaller than the bottom digit, take a 1 from the digit in the column to the left and write it next to the digit you are subtracting from.

Cross out the digit you took the 1 from and write it out as 1 less. Now you can subtract.

```
   ³4̸ ¹5
  - 3 8
  _____
       7
```

```
    2 ⁶7̸ ¹4
  -   3 5
  _____
    2 3 9
```

Decimal Subtraction

Decimal subtraction uses the same rules as column subtraction. You may need to exchange.

Step 1 Write the question out with the decimal points in the same column so the place value is clear. You may need to add place-holding zeros.

Example: 14 - 9.27 = ?

```
1 4 · 0 0
  9 · 2 7
_____
      ·
```

Step 2 Start in the column with the smallest place value. Subtract the bottom number from the top. You might need to regroup, perhaps even more than once.

```
1 ³4̶ · ¹0 0                1 ³4̶ · ̶0̶⁹ ¹0
  9 · 2 7         ➞            9 · 2 7
_____                 _____
      ·                          ·     3
```

Step 3 Move on to subtracting in the next column to the left, regrouping where needed. Do this for every column.

```
⁰1̶ ¹³4̶ · ̶0̶⁹ ¹0          14 - 9.27 = 4.73
   9 · 2 7
_____
   4 · 7 3
```

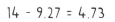

Multiplication & Division

Multiplication & Division Vocabulary

MULTIPLICATION: X

multiply	double	groups of
times	triple	multiplied by
twice	product	

Parts of Multiplication

$$5 \times 3 = 15$$

factor   operator   factor   product

DIVISION: ÷

divided by	divide	groups
shared by	equally	remainder

Parts of Division

$$20 \div 4 = 5$$

dividend   operator   divisor   quotient

Times Tables: x 1, x 2, x 5

1 times table – Multiplying any number by 1 does not change it, e.g. 5 x 1 = 5.

0 x 1 = 0	5 x 1 = 5	9 x 1 = 9
1 x 1 = 1	6 x 1 = 6	10 x 1 = 10
2 x 1 = 2	7 x 1 = 7	11 x 1 = 11
3 x 1 = 3	8 x 1 = 8	12 x 1 = 12
4 x 1 = 4		

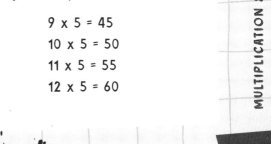

Multiplying a number by 0 always = 0. E.g. 5 x 0 = 0.

2 times table – Multiplying a number by 2 doubles it, e.g. 5 x 2 = 10; double 5 is 10.

0 x 2 = 0	5 x 2 = 10	9 x 2 = 18
1 x 2 = 2	6 x 2 = 12	10 x 2 = 20
2 x 2 = 4	7 x 2 = 14	11 x 2 = 22
3 x 2 = 6	8 x 2 = 16	12 x 2 = 24
4 x 2 = 8		

5 times table – All multiples of 5 end in either a 5 or a 0. If you multiply an odd number by 5, the product ends in 5. If you multiply an even number by 5, the product ends in 0.

0 x 5 = 0	5 x 5 = 25	9 x 5 = 45
1 x 5 = 5	6 x 5 = 30	10 x 5 = 50
2 x 5 = 10	7 x 5 = 35	11 x 5 = 55
3 x 5 = 15	8 x 5 = 40	12 x 5 = 60
4 x 5 = 20		

Times Tables: x 10, x 3, x 4

10 times table – All multiples of 10 end in 0.

0 x 10 = 0	5 x 10 = 50	9 x 10 = 90
1 x 10 = 10	6 x 10 = 60	10 x 10 = 100
2 x 10 = 20	7 x 10 = 70	11 x 10 = 110
3 x 10 = 30	8 x 10 = 80	12 x 10 = 120
4 x 10 = 40		

3 times table – The digits of numbers in the 3 times table add up to multiples of 3. In the number 24, the digits 2 and 4 add up to 6, which is a multiple of 3.

0 x 3 = 0	5 x 3 = 15	9 x 3 = 27
1 x 3 = 3	6 x 3 = 18	10 x 3 = 30
2 x 3 = 6	7 x 3 = 21	11 x 3 = 33
3 x 3 = 9	8 x 3 = 24	12 x 3 = 36
4 x 3 = 12		

4 times table – The 4 times table is double the 2 times table, e.g. 3 x 2 = 6 and 3 x 4 = 12.

0 x 4 = 0	5 x 4 = 20	9 x 4 = 36
1 x 4 = 4	6 x 4 = 24	10 x 4 = 40
2 x 4 = 8	7 x 4 = 28	11 x 4 = 44
3 x 4 = 12	8 x 4 = 32	12 x 4 = 48
4 x 4 = 16		

Times Tables: x 6, x 7, x 8

6 times table – The 6 times table is double the 3 times table, e.g. 4 x 3 = 12 and 4 x 6 = 24.

0 x 6 = 0	5 x 6 = 30	9 x 6 = 54
1 x 6 = 6	6 x 6 = 36	10 x 6 = 60
2 x 6 = 12	7 x 6 = 42	11 x 6 = 66
3 x 6 = 18	8 x 6 = 48	12 x 6 = 72
4 x 6 = 24		

7 times table – Numbers in the 7 times table can be found by combining numbers in the 5 and 2 times tables. 7 x 8 = 56, 8 x 5 = 40 and 8 x 2 = 16. The sum of 40 and 16 is 56.

0 x 7 = 0	5 x 7 = 35	9 x 7 = 63
1 x 7 = 7	6 x 7 = 42	10 x 7 = 70
2 x 7 = 14	7 x 7 = 49	11 x 7 = 77
3 x 7 = 21	8 x 7 = 56	12 x 7 = 84
4 x 7 = 28		

8 times table – The 8 times table is double the 4 times table, e.g. 3 x 4 = 12 and 3 x 8 = 24. You can add 8 to a number more easily by adding 10 and then subtracting 2.

0 x 8 = 0	5 x 8 = 40	9 x 8 = 72
1 x 8 = 8	6 x 8 = 48	10 x 8 = 80
2 x 8 = 16	7 x 8 = 56	11 x 8 = 88
3 x 8 = 24	8 x 8 = 64	12 x 8 = 96
4 x 8 = 32		

Times Tables: x 9, x 11, x 12

9 times table – The digits in all multiples of 9 add up to 9:
e.g. 5 x 9 = 45   4 + 5 = 9

0 x 9 = 0	5 x 9 = 45	9 x 9 = 81
1 x 9 = 9	6 x 9 = 54	10 x 9 = 90
2 x 9 = 18	7 x 9 = 63	11 x 9 = 99
3 x 9 = 27	8 x 9 = 72	12 x 9 = 108
4 x 9 = 36		

11 times table – All the multiples of 11 under 100 have the
same tens digit and ones digit: e.g. 5 x 11 = 55.

0 x 11 = 0	5 x 11 = 55	9 x 11 = 99
1 x 11 = 11	6 x 11 = 66	10 x 11 = 110
2 x 11 = 22	7 x 11 = 77	11 x 11 = 121
3 x 11 = 33	8 x 11 = 88	12 x 11 = 132
4 x 11 = 44		

12 times table – Multiplying by 10 and by 2 separately can
be easier than multiplying by 12: e.g. 2 x 10 = 20 + 2 x 2 =4.
So, 2 x 12 = 24 (20 + 4)

0 x 12 = 0	5 x 12 = 60	9 x 12 = 108
1 x 12 = 12	6 x 12 = 72	10 x 12 = 120
2 x 12 = 24	7 x 12 = 84	11 x 12 = 132
3 x 12 = 36	8 x 12 = 96	12 x 12 = 144
4 x 12 = 48		

Division Facts

$1 \div 1 = 1$	$2 \div 2 = 1$	$5 \div 5 = 1$
$2 \div 1 = 2$	$4 \div 2 = 2$	$10 \div 5 = 2$
$3 \div 1 = 3$	$6 \div 2 = 3$	$15 \div 5 = 3$
$4 \div 1 = 4$	$8 \div 2 = 4$	$20 \div 5 = 4$
$5 \div 1 = 5$	$10 \div 2 = 5$	$25 \div 5 = 5$
$6 \div 1 = 6$	$12 \div 2 = 6$	$30 \div 5 = 6$
$7 \div 1 = 7$	$14 \div 2 = 7$	$35 \div 5 = 7$
$8 \div 1 = 8$	$16 \div 2 = 8$	$40 \div 5 = 8$
$9 \div 1 = 9$	$18 \div 2 = 9$	$45 \div 5 = 9$
$10 \div 1 = 10$	$20 \div 2 = 10$	$50 \div 5 = 10$
$11 \div 1 = 11$	$22 \div 2 = 11$	$55 \div 5 = 11$
$12 \div 1 = 12$	$24 \div 2 = 12$	$60 \div 5 = 12$

$10 \div 10 = 1$	$3 \div 3 = 1$	$4 \div 4 = 1$
$20 \div 10 = 2$	$6 \div 3 = 2$	$8 \div 4 = 2$
$30 \div 10 = 3$	$9 \div 3 = 3$	$12 \div 4 = 3$
$40 \div 10 = 4$	$12 \div 3 = 4$	$16 \div 4 = 4$
$50 \div 10 = 5$	$15 \div 3 = 5$	$20 \div 4 = 5$
$60 \div 10 = 6$	$18 \div 3 = 6$	$24 \div 4 = 6$
$70 \div 10 = 7$	$21 \div 3 = 7$	$28 \div 4 = 7$
$80 \div 10 = 8$	$24 \div 3 = 8$	$32 \div 4 = 8$
$90 \div 10 = 9$	$27 \div 3 = 9$	$36 \div 4 = 9$
$100 \div 10 = 10$	$30 \div 3 = 10$	$40 \div 4 = 10$
$110 \div 10 = 11$	$33 \div 3 = 11$	$44 \div 4 = 11$
$120 \div 10 = 12$	$36 \div 3 = 12$	$48 \div 4 = 12$

Division Facts

6 ÷ 6 = 1	7 ÷ 7 = 1	8 ÷ 8 = 1
12 ÷ 6 = 2	14 ÷ 7 = 2	16 ÷ 8 = 2
18 ÷ 6 = 3	21 ÷ 7 = 3	24 ÷ 8 = 3
24 ÷ 6 = 4	28 ÷ 7 = 4	32 ÷ 8 = 4
30 ÷ 6 = 5	35 ÷ 7 = 5	40 ÷ 8 = 5
36 ÷ 6 = 6	42 ÷ 7 = 6	48 ÷ 8 = 6
42 ÷ 6 = 7	49 ÷ 7 = 7	56 ÷ 8 = 7
48 ÷ 6 = 8	56 ÷ 7 = 8	64 ÷ 8 = 8
54 ÷ 6 = 9	63 ÷ 7 = 9	72 ÷ 8 = 9
60 ÷ 6 = 10	70 ÷ 7 = 10	80 ÷ 8 = 10
66 ÷ 6 = 11	77 ÷ 7 = 11	88 ÷ 8 = 11
72 ÷ 6 = 12	84 ÷ 7 = 12	96 ÷ 8 = 12

9 ÷ 9 = 1	11 ÷ 11 = 1	12 ÷ 12 = 1
18 ÷ 9 = 2	22 ÷ 11 = 2	24 ÷ 12 = 2
27 ÷ 9 = 3	33 ÷ 11 = 3	36 ÷ 12 = 3
36 ÷ 9 = 4	44 ÷ 11 = 4	48 ÷ 12 = 4
45 ÷ 9 = 5	55 ÷ 11 = 5	60 ÷ 12 = 5
54 ÷ 9 = 6	66 ÷ 11 = 6	72 ÷ 12 = 6
63 ÷ 9 = 7	77 ÷ 11 = 7	84 ÷ 12 = 7
72 ÷ 9 = 8	88 ÷ 11 = 8	96 ÷ 12 = 8
81 ÷ 9 = 9	99 ÷ 11 = 9	108 ÷ 12 = 9
90 ÷ 9 = 10	110 ÷ 11 = 10	120 ÷ 12 = 10
99 ÷ 9 = 11	121 ÷ 11 = 11	132 ÷ 12 = 11
108 ÷ 9 = 12	132 ÷ 11 = 12	144 ÷ 12 = 12

Arrays

Arrays show a multiplication problem in picture form. Simply arrange the numbers from the multiplication in rows and columns.

So for example, if you have 3 x 4, you could create 3 rows of 4, or 4 rows of 3. Count the dots and find the total.

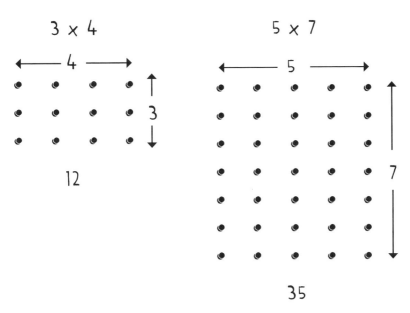

3 x 4

12

5 x 7

35

NINJA TIP:

Remember, multiplication is **communicative**. This means you can multiply the factors either way and still get the same answer, such as 3 x 4 = 12, 4 x 3 = 12.

Multiplication: Repeated Addition

Step 1
Draw a number line beginning with zero.

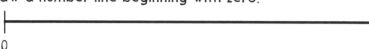

0

Step 2
Repeatedly add your chosen factor, making notes of your jumps and the ongoing total. This is repeated addition.

Example 1: 4 x 5 = ?

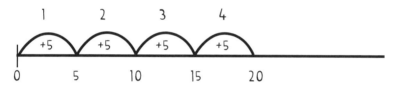

Example 2: 6 x 3 = ?

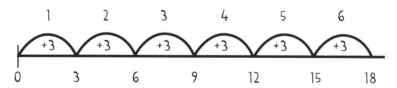

NINJA TIP:

Choose to repeatedly add a number that you are confident adding.
For example, for 8 x 3 adding 3 might be easier than adding 8.

Grid / Partition Multiplication

Step 1 Partition the two-digit or three-digit factor into ones, tens and hundred values. Write these down the left-hand side of the grid. Write the other factor at the top.

Example 1:

$3 \times 26 = ?$

	3
20	
6	

Example 2:

$4 \times 132 = ?$

	4
100	
30	
2	

Step 2 Multiply each number on the left-hand side by the top factor. Write the total in the corresponding row.

Example 1:

$3 \times 26 = ?$

	3
20	6 0
6	1 8

Example 2:

$4 \times 132 = ?$

	4
100	4 0 0
30	1 2 0
2	8

Write the place value accurately.

Step 3 Total the values of each multiplication, using a mental addition strategy or column addition.

Example 1:

$60 + 18 = 78$

So, $3 \times 26 = 78$

Example 2

$4 \times 132 = 528$

```
   4 0 0
 +1 2 0
 +     8
 ───────
   5 2 8
```

Short Multiplication

Step 1 Set out the calculation with the biggest number on top and align the digits. Write the multiplication operator.

2-digit example: 4 x 27 = **?**

```
    2 7
x     4
_____
```

3-digit example: 5 x 342 = **?**

```
    3 4 2
x       5
_____
```

Step 2 Multiply the top number by the bottom number. First multiply the ones, then the tens, then the hundreds. You can jot these down if needed.

O: 7 x 4 = 28
T: 2o x 4 = 80

O: 2 x 5 = 10
T: 4o x 5 = 200
H: 300 x 5 = 1,500

Step 3 Only a single digit can be placed in each column of the answer space. You will need to carry digits to the next column if necessary.

```
    2 7
x     4
_____
  1 0 8
  1 2
```

```
    3 4 2
x       5
_____
  1 7 1 0
  1 2 1
```

NINJA TIP:
Don't forget to add the digits that you carry.

Expanded Short Multiplication

The expanded method of short multiplication helps us to fully see each calculation as we carry it out.

Example 1: 5 x 126 = ?

```
    1 2 6
  x     5
  ─────────
      3 0   (= 5 x 6)
    1 0 0   (= 5 x 20)
    5 0 0   (= 5 x 100)
  ─────────
    6 3 0
```

Example 2: 3 x 245 = ?

```
    2 4 5
  x     3
  ─────────
      1 5   (= 3 x 5)
    1 2 0   (= 3 x 40)
    6 0 0   (= 3 x 200)
  ─────────
    7 3 5
```

Long Multiplication

Step 1 Write out the question with the biggest number on top. Example: 24 x 35 = ?

```
    3 5
x   2 4
_____
```

Step 2 Multiply the top digits by the ones on the bottom row. Start with the top ones column x bottom ones column. Then repeat for the top tens, top hundreds and so on.

```
      3 5
x     2 4
_____
    1 4 0   (5 x 4 = 20, 3 x 4 = 12)
      2 ←
```

Step 3 Write 0 in the ones column of the second answer row – this is needed because you are now multiplying by 10. Multiply the numbers on the top row by the tens on the bottom row. Start with the top ones column x bottom tens column.

```
      3 5
x     2 4
_____
    1 4 0
    7 0 (0)   (5 x 2 = 10, 3 x 2 = 6)
    1 2
```

This place-holding zero will help you keep the place value accurate.

Step 4 Add up both answer rows using column addition.

24 x 35 = 840

```
      3 5
x     2 4
_____
    1 4 0
+   7 0 0
_____
    8 4 0
```

Decimal Multiplication

Short Multiplication with Decimals

This is carried out in the same way as short multiplication.
The key is to ensure the place value is correct.

Example: 4 x 2.36 = ?

```
    2 . 3 6
  x       4
  ─────────
    9 . 4 4
    1   2
```

Long Multiplication with Decimals

The rules and the strategy for long multiplication still
apply when working with decimals. Don't forget your place
holding zero when you multiply by the tens column.

Example: 16 x 3.42 = ?

```
      3 . 4 2
  x     1 6
  ───────────
  2 ²0 . ¹5 2
  3 4 . 2 0
  ───────────
  5 4 . 7 2
```

NINJA TIP:

Ensure that the decimal point
in the question is in the same
column as the decimal
point in the answer.
Try to do this when you
write out the question.
This will mean that
the place value of
the question is correct!

Multiplication: Partition & Jot

Partition and jot is a great strategy to jot down your mental calculations quickly and easily.

Step 1 Jot down the question.

2-digit example: 4 x 26 = ?   **3-digit example: 3 x 149 = ?**

Step 2 Partition (separate) the two-digit or three-digit numbers into their hundreds, tens and ones values. Then multiply each part individually.

	2 0	6
x 4		x 4
	8 0	2 4

	1 0 0	4 0	9
x 3	x 3	x 3	
	3 0 0	1 2 0	2 7

Step 3 Add the parts together, jotting as you go.

80 + 24 = 104   300 + 120 + 27 = 447

4 x 26 = 104   **3 x 149 = 447**

NINJA TIP:

The reason we make jottings as we go is so that we don't need to hold this information in our head. It's already been jotted down.

Division Strategy: Grouping

Step 1 Write out the dots until you have the number you are dividing (the dividend).

Example with no remainder: 15 ÷ 3 =?

o o o o o o o o o o o o o o o

Example with remainder: 13 ÷ 3 =?

o o o o o o o o o o o o o

Step 2 Draw circles to group the dots by the number you are dividing by (the divisor).

15 ÷ 3 =?

(o o o)(o o o)(o o o)(o o o)(o o o)

13 ÷ 3 =?

(o o o)(o o o)(o o o)(o o o)o

Step 3 Count the number of groups you circled. Any dots left over are remainders as there aren't enough to form a complete group.

5 groups, so 15 ÷ 3 = 5

(o o o)(o o o)(o o o)(o o o)(o o o)

4 groups with 1 dot remaining, so 13 ÷ 3 = 4 remainder 1

(o o o)(o o o)(o o o)(o o o)o

Short Division

Step 1 Write the question out as below.

$212 \div 4 = ?$

$$4\ \overline{\big)\ 2\ 1\ 2}$$

Step 2 Start with the highest place value digit. See if it can be divided by the divisor. If it can, write the answer above the line. If it can't, cross out the digit and carry it over to the next column. Then repeat this step.

$$4\ \overline{\big)\ \cancel{2}\ {}^2 1\ 2}\quad {}^5$$

2 can't be divided by 4. So carry the 2 over to the tens column, next to the 1. $21 \div 4 = 5$ r 1. Write 5 above and carry the 1 to the ones column.

$$4\ \overline{\big)\ \cancel{2}\ {}^2 1\ {}^1 2}\quad {}^{5\ 3}$$

12 divided by 4 is 3. So write 3 above. $212 \div 4 = 53$

Step 3 If there is a remainder when you divide the smallest place value, then this is part of your answer.

$$6\ \overline{\big)\ \cancel{2}\ {}^2 0\ {}^2 6}\quad {}^{3\ 4}\ \ r\ 2$$

Example with remainder:
$206 \div 6 = 34$ r 2

NINJA TIP:

Short division is most often used when dividing by a one-digit number.

Division Strategy: Number Line

Step 1 Draw a vertical number line with zero at the bottom.

Example: **35 ÷ 7 = ?**

Step 2 Count in steps of the number you're dividing by (divisor) up to the number you're dividing (dividend). The answer is the number of steps (5).

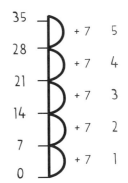

Combined Steps You can use larger chunks and fewer steps. Instead of 10 steps of 7, you might know that 10 x 7 = 70.

Step 1 Draw a number line.

Example: **94 ÷ 7 = ?**

Step 2 Choose a multiple of the divisor as a larger chunk. Count up using this. Note how many times the divisor goes into the chunk.

Step 3 If that chunk is too big to count up again, choose smaller chunks until you reach the dividend. The answer is the total of how many times the divisor goes into the chunks (13 r 3).

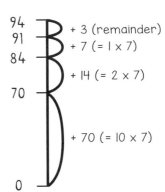

NINJA TIP:

If adding the divisor one more time isn't possible but you haven't reached the dividend, the difference between where you got to and the dividend is the remainder.

Long Division

Step 1 Write the question out as in the examples below.

2-digit example: 57 ÷ 3 = **?**   3-digit example: 194 ÷ 6 = **?**

```
3 | 5 7                6 | 1 9 4
```

Step 2 Subtract multiples of the divisor from the dividend. In brackets, write how many lots of the divisor are in the chunk.

```
  3 | 5 7                  6 | 1 9 4
-     3 0  (10 x 3)      -     6 0  (10 x 6)
      ———                      ———
      2 7                      1 3 4
```

Step 3 Repeat until you can no longer subtract the divisor.

```
  3 | 5 7                  6 | 1 9 4
-     3 0  (10 x 3)      -     6 0  (10 x 6)
      ———                      ———
      2 7                      1 3 4
-     2 7  (9 x 3)       -     1 2 0  (20 x 6)
      ———                      ———
      0                        1 4
                        -       1 2  (2 x 6)
                                ———
                                2
```

Step 4 Add up how many lots of the divisor you used from your notes in brackets. This is the answer. Anything left over is a remainder (r): this value is less than the divisor.

10 + 9 = 19, 57 ÷ 3 = 19   10 + 20 + 2 = 32, 194 ÷ 6 = 32 r 2

Long Division: Partial Tables

Partial tables help you work with numbers you might not know the times tables for. With a partial table, we can easily calculate x 1, x 2, x 4, x 10 and x 5.

Step 1 Draw a table like this. List 1, 2, 4, 10 and 5 in that order in the lefthand column. Write the divisor at the top (we've used 14 here).

x	14
1	
2	
4	
10	
5	

Step 2 Calculate the totals for x 1, x 2 and x 4.
1 x 14 = 14, 2 x 14 = 28, etc.

x	14
1	14
2	28
4	56
10	
5	

x 2
x 2

Step 3 Fill in x 10. Then halve the answer to get x 5.

x	14
1	14
2	28
4	56
10	140
5	70

x 2
x 2
÷ 2

NINJA TIP:

See the next page for how to use partial tables for division. It works best when dividing by a two-digit number.

Long Division: Partial Tables

Use partial tables with long division to answer division sums.

Fill in the table. Then use the long division method (page 53). Use your answers in the partial table to help you decide which chunks to subtract away from the dividend.

Remember to write in brackets how many lots of the divisor are in the chunk. You already have this number in the lefthand column in the partial table.

Example: 672 ÷ 16 = ?

	16
1	16
2	32
4	64
10	160
5	80

× 2
× 2
÷ 2

```
            4  2
   16 | 6  7  2
   -     6  4  0   (40 × 16)
            3  2
   -        3  2   (2 × 16)
               0
```

You can use the partial table to find even bigger chunks. Example: here we've taken 4 × 16 = 64 and made it 10 x bigger — 40 × 16 = 640. This helps you solve the question more quickly.

4 Fractions, Decimals & Percentages

Fractions, Decimals & Percentages

$\frac{1}{1} = 1.0 = 100\%$									
$\frac{1}{2} = 0.5 = 50\%$					$\frac{1}{2} = 0.5 = 50\%$				
$\frac{1}{4} = 0.25 = 25\%$		$\frac{1}{4} = 0.25 = 25\%$		$\frac{1}{4} = 0.25 = 25\%$		$\frac{1}{4} = 0.25 = 25\%$			
$\frac{1}{8}$ = 0.125 = 12.5%	$\frac{1}{8}$ = 0.125 = 12.5%	$\frac{1}{8}$ = 0.125 = 12.5%	$\frac{1}{8}$ = 0.125 = 12.5%	$\frac{1}{8}$ = 0.125 = 12.5%	$\frac{1}{8}$ = 0.125 = 12.5%	$\frac{1}{8}$ = 0.125 = 12.5%	$\frac{1}{8}$ = 0.125 = 12.5%		
$\frac{1}{5} = 0.20 = 20\%$		$\frac{1}{5} = 0.20 = 20\%$		$\frac{1}{5} = 0.20 = 20\%$		$\frac{1}{5} = 0.20 = 20\%$		$\frac{1}{5} = 0.20 = 20\%$	
$\frac{1}{10}$ = 0.10 = 10%	$\frac{1}{10}$ = 0.10 = 10%	$\frac{1}{10}$ = 0.10 = 10%	$\frac{1}{10}$ = 0.10 = 10%	$\frac{1}{10}$ = 0.10 = 10%	$\frac{1}{10}$ = 0.10 = 10%	$\frac{1}{10}$ = 0.10 = 10%	$\frac{1}{10}$ = 0.10 = 10%	$\frac{1}{10}$ = 0.10 = 10%	$\frac{1}{10}$ = 0.10 = 10%

57

Fractions Basics

A fraction is used to represent parts of a whole.
A fraction is made up of a numerator, a fraction bar
and a denominator.

numerator ⟶ **1**

fraction bar ⟶ **——**

denominator ⟶ **2**

The numerator is how many equal
parts of the whole we have.

The denominator is how many equal
parts the whole is made up of.

Different ways to represent fractions

Part of a Group

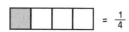 $= \frac{1}{4}$

Number Line

Bar Model

$= \frac{1}{4}$

Circle

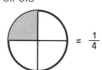 $= \frac{1}{4}$

Key Vocabulary:

whole
part
half
quarter
numerator
denominator

NINJA TIP:

Knowing your times tables makes working with
fractions much easier!

58

Equivalent Fractions

Halves: A half as a fraction is written as $\frac{1}{2}$. But it can also be shown as $\frac{2}{4}$, $\frac{3}{6}$, $\frac{4}{8}$ and others. These are known as equivalent fractions – they equal each other.

Remember, 'half' means something being split or shared into or by two. So when referring to a half, think about how the whole has been split into 2 equal parts.

Quarters: A quarter as a fraction is written as $\frac{1}{4}$, but it can also be shown as $\frac{2}{8}$, $\frac{3}{12}$, $\frac{4}{16}$ and others. These are equivalent fractions to $\frac{1}{4}$.

Remember, a quarter means something being split or shared into four. So when referring to a quarter, think about how the whole has been split into 4 equal parts.

  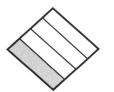

Equivalent Fractions

Equivalent fractions are fractions that are equal in value, but have different numerators and denominators.

$\frac{2}{4}$ $\frac{3}{6}$ $\frac{4}{8}$ $\frac{8}{16}$ $\frac{12}{24}$ are all equivalent to a half.

$\frac{2}{8}$ $\frac{3}{12}$ $\frac{5}{20}$ $\frac{6}{24}$ are all equivalent to a quarter.

$\frac{2}{10}$ $\frac{3}{15}$ $\frac{4}{20}$ $\frac{10}{50}$ are all equivalent to a fifth.

The fractions remain equal because if you multiply or divide both the numerator and denominator by the same number, they increase or decrease by the same value.

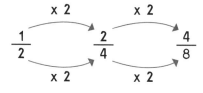

Visually it looks like this:

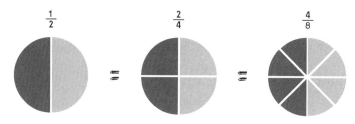

Simplifying Fractions

When working with fractions, you may be asked to simplify a fraction. This means to make the denominator as small a value as possible.

To simplify a fraction, you need to divide the numerator and the denominator by the same number.

So you need to find numbers that both the numerator and denominator can be divided by.

Using divide by 2:

$\frac{16}{32} \longrightarrow \frac{8}{16} \longrightarrow \frac{4}{8} \longrightarrow \frac{2}{4} \longrightarrow \frac{1}{2}$

Using divide by 4:

$\frac{16}{32} \longrightarrow \frac{4}{8} \longrightarrow \frac{1}{2}$

Using divide by 16:

$\frac{16}{32} \longrightarrow \frac{1}{2}$

Or use a mix of numbers – if you can't divide again by the same number, try another smaller one.

Using divide by 8, then by 2:

$\frac{16}{32} \longrightarrow \frac{2}{4} \longrightarrow \frac{1}{2}$

NINJA TIP:

If you are struggling to simplify a fraction, keep dividing by 2 until you can't divide it into a whole number.

NINJA TIP:

The larger the number you find that divides into both the numerator and the denominator, the quicker you can simplify a fraction.

Add & Subtract Fractions

Adding and subtracting fractions with the same denominator is very simple.

When we add or subtract fractions with the same denominator, the denominator stays the same, while the numerator increases or decreases.

Addition examples:

$\frac{1}{4}$ + $\frac{1}{4}$ = $\frac{2}{4}$

$\frac{2}{7} + \frac{3}{7} = \frac{5}{7}$

$\frac{6}{13} + \frac{4}{13} = \frac{10}{13}$

Subtraction examples:

$\frac{2}{4}$ − $\frac{1}{4}$ = $\frac{1}{4}$

$\frac{5}{6} - \frac{2}{6} = \frac{3}{6}$

$\frac{8}{9} - \frac{6}{9} = \frac{2}{9}$

Add & Subtract Fractions

To add and subtract fractions with different denominators, you first need to change the denominators to be the same.

To do this, you find a common multiple (a number in the times tables of both denominators), then change them both to this number. This is called a common denominator.

Example: $\frac{1}{3} + \frac{1}{4} = ?$ Times table for 3: 3, 6, 9, ⑫ 15
Times table for 4: 4, 8, ⑫ 16, 20

For 3 to become 12 we multiply by 4, so multiply the numerator by 4 as well. For 4 to become 12 we multiply by 3, so multiply the numerator by 3 as well.

Re-write the question with 12 as the common denominator for both fractions and with the new numerators.

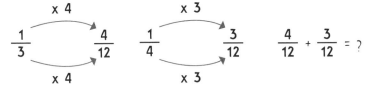

$$\frac{1}{3} \xrightarrow{\times 4} \frac{4}{12} \qquad \frac{1}{4} \xrightarrow{\times 3} \frac{3}{12} \qquad \frac{4}{12} + \frac{3}{12} = ?$$

Now simply add or subtract the numerators.

$$\frac{4}{12} + \frac{3}{12} = \frac{7}{12} \qquad\qquad \frac{1}{3} + \frac{1}{4} = \frac{7}{12}$$

NINJA TIP:

Sometimes denominators have more than one common multiple. Try to use the lowest one. This is called the lowest common multiple.

Comparing & Ordering Fractions

Comparing fractions

We compare fractions by seeing if they are smaller, larger or the same size. This is easier if the denominators are the same. If they are different, find a common denominator for the two fractions and adjust them (see page 63).

Example: Which fraction is larger? $\frac{5}{8}$ or $\frac{4}{6}$?

$\times 3 \Big(\frac{\frac{5}{8}}{\frac{15}{24}} \quad \times 4 \Big(\frac{\frac{4}{6}}{\frac{16}{24}}$

Once the fractions are adjusted, it is easy to compare them. $\frac{16}{24}$ is bigger than $\frac{15}{24}$. $\frac{4}{6}$ is bigger than $\frac{5}{8}$.

Ordering fractions

Ordering fractions is the same as comparing fractions, only there are more fractions to work with. You may be asked to order a set of fractions from smallest to largest.

Example: Order $\frac{1}{2}$, $\frac{3}{4}$, $\frac{4}{6}$ and $\frac{5}{12}$ from smallest to largest.

$\times 6 \Big(\frac{\frac{1}{2}}{\frac{6}{12}} \quad \times 3 \Big(\frac{\frac{3}{4}}{\frac{9}{12}} \quad \times 2 \Big(\frac{\frac{4}{6}}{\frac{8}{12}} \quad \Big(\frac{\frac{5}{12}}{\frac{5}{12}}$ no need to adjust

In order: $\frac{5}{12}$, $\frac{6}{12}$, $\frac{8}{12}$, $\frac{9}{12}$. The answer is $\frac{5}{12}$, $\frac{1}{2}$, $\frac{4}{6}$, $\frac{3}{4}$.

NINJA TIP:

When writing your final answer, use the original fractions in the question, not the fractions you adjusted.

Improper Fractions & Mixed Numbers

Improper fractions have a numerator bigger than the denominator – the fraction is more than a whole, for example $\frac{6}{5}$. $\frac{5}{5}$ is a whole.

Proper fractions have a numerator smaller than the denominator - the fraction is less than a whole, for example $\frac{4}{5}$. $\frac{5}{5}$ is a whole.

A **mixed number** is a whole number and a fraction.

To convert an improper fraction to a mixed number:

Step 1 Divide the numerator by the denominator.

$\frac{7}{5}$ = 7 ÷ 5 = 1 r 2 (there's one whole 5 in 7, with 2 left)

Step 2 The first part of the answer is the whole number in the mixed number. To make the fraction part, write the remainder as the numerator over the original denominator.

$\frac{7}{5}$ = 7 ÷ 5 = 1 r 2 = $1\frac{2}{5}$ $\frac{7}{5}$ = $1\frac{2}{5}$

To convert a mixed number to an improper fraction:

Step 1 Multiply the whole number part of the mixed number by the denominator from the fraction part to make the whole number into a fraction.

Example: $2\frac{1}{4}$ 2 x 4 = 8, so 2 = $\frac{8}{4}$

Step 2 Add the result to the fraction part of the mixed number. This is the new improper fraction.

$\frac{8}{4}$ + $\frac{1}{4}$ = $\frac{9}{4}$ Answer: $2\frac{1}{4}$ = $\frac{9}{4}$

Multiplying Proper Fractions

Multiplying proper fractions together is very simple.

All you need to do is multiply the numerators together to get a new numerator.

Then multiply the denominators to get a new denominator.

Example: What is $\dfrac{3}{4} \times \dfrac{2}{5}$?

$$\dfrac{3}{4} \times \dfrac{2}{5} \quad \overset{3 \times 2}{\underset{4 \times 5}{\longrightarrow}} \quad = \dfrac{6}{20} \qquad \dfrac{6}{20} \ \overset{\div 2}{\underset{\div 2}{\text{simplified}}} \ \dfrac{3}{10}$$

$$\dfrac{3}{4} \times \dfrac{2}{5} = \dfrac{6}{20} \text{ or } \dfrac{3}{10}$$

NINJA TIP:

It is a good habit to simplify fractions where possible, see page 61 for how to do this.

Multiplying & Dividing Proper Fractions by Whole Numbers

Multiplying proper fractions by a whole number

To multiply a proper fraction by a whole number, multiply the numerator by the whole number to get your new numerator. The denominator stays the same.

Example: $\dfrac{2}{6} \times 2 = ?$ $\dfrac{2}{6} \xrightarrow{\times 2} \dfrac{4}{6}$ $\dfrac{2}{6} \times 2 = \dfrac{4}{6}$

Sometimes you might multiply a fraction and finish with an improper fraction. Be sure to convert this improper fraction into a mixed number (see page 65).

Example: $\dfrac{2}{4} \times 5 = ?$ $\dfrac{2}{4} \times 5 = \dfrac{10}{4}$ ($\dfrac{10}{4}$ is improper.)

How many 4s in 10? 2 with 2 remainder. $\dfrac{2}{4} \times 5 = 2\dfrac{2}{4}$

Dividing proper fractions by a whole number

To divide a proper fraction by a whole number, multiply the denominator by the whole number to get your new denominator. Your numerator stays the same.

Example: $\dfrac{2}{6} \div 2 = ?$ $\dfrac{2}{6} \xrightarrow[\times 2]{} \dfrac{2}{12}$ $\dfrac{2}{6} \div 2 = \dfrac{2}{12}$

67

Multiplying Mixed Numbers by Whole Numbers

Method 1: Convert to an improper fraction

Step 1 Multiply the denominator (4) by the whole number (2), then add the numerator (1).

$$Q: 2\frac{1}{4} \times 3 = ? \qquad 4 \times 2 + 1 = 9 \qquad 2\frac{1}{4} = \frac{9}{4}$$

Step 2 Multiply the improper fraction by the whole number (numerator x whole number).

$$\frac{9}{4} \times 3 = \frac{27}{4}$$

Step 3 Convert the new improper fraction to a mixed number. Divide the numerator by the denominator to get the whole number. The remainder is your new numerator. The denominator is the same as the original mixed number.

$$27 \div 4 = 6 \text{ r } 3 \qquad \frac{27}{4} = 6\frac{3}{4} \qquad Q: 2\frac{1}{4} \times 3 = 6\frac{3}{4}$$

Method 2: Partition the mixed number

Step 1 Partition the whole number and the proper fraction.

$$Q: 2\frac{1}{4} \times 3 = ? \qquad 2\frac{1}{4} \longrightarrow 2 \qquad \frac{1}{4}$$

Step 2 Multiply both parts by the whole number (3).

$$2 \times 3 = 6 \qquad \frac{1}{4} \times 3 = \frac{3}{4}$$

Step 3 Add the two parts together. This is your answer.

$$6 + \frac{3}{4} = 6\frac{3}{4} \qquad Q: 2\frac{1}{4} \times 3 = 6\frac{3}{4}$$

Adding & Subtracting Mixed Numbers

Method 1: Convert to an improper fraction

NINJA TIP: To do this, find a common denominator — see page 64.

Step 1 Convert both mixed numbers to improper fractions.

Example: $2\frac{1}{3} + 1\frac{1}{2} = ?$

See page 65 for this.

$2\frac{1}{3} = \frac{7}{3}$ $\qquad$ $1\frac{1}{2} = \frac{3}{2}$

Step 2 Find the lowest common denominator of the two improper fractions. It's 6.

$3 \times 2 = 6$

$2 \times 3 = 6$

Step 3 Multiply the numerator of each fraction by the same amount as the denominator has been multiplied.

$\frac{7}{3}$ $\begin{array}{c} \times 2 \\ \times 2 \end{array}$ $\frac{14}{6}$ $\qquad$ $\frac{3}{2}$ $\begin{array}{c} \times 3 \\ \times 3 \end{array}$ $\frac{9}{6}$

Step 4 Add the fractions together.

$\frac{14}{6} + \frac{9}{6} = \frac{23}{6}$

Step 5 Convert back to a mixed number.

$\frac{23}{6} = 3\frac{5}{6}$

NINJA TIP:

This works in exactly the same way for subtraction too.

Adding & Subtracting Mixed Numbers

Method 2: Partition the mixed numbers

Step 1 Partition (separate) the whole numbers from the fractions.

This works in the same way for subtraction.

Example: $2\frac{1}{3} + 1\frac{1}{2} = ?$ (2) $\frac{1}{3}$ (1) $\frac{1}{2}$

whole numbers

Step 2 Add the whole numbers. $2 + 1 = 3$

Step 3 Find the lowest common denominator of the two proper fractions. It's 6.

$3 \times 2 = 6$

$2 \times 3 = 6$

Step 4 Multiply the numerator of each fraction by the same amount as the denominator has been multiplied.

$\frac{1}{3}$ $\begin{matrix} \times 2 \\ \times 2 \end{matrix}$ $\frac{2}{6}$ $\frac{1}{2}$ $\begin{matrix} \times 3 \\ \times 3 \end{matrix}$ $\frac{3}{6}$

Step 5 Add the fractions together.

$\frac{2}{6} + \frac{3}{6} = \frac{5}{6}$

Step 6 Don't forget to add the whole number total from Step 2 to the final mixed number.

$3 + \frac{5}{6} = 3\frac{5}{6}$ $2\frac{1}{3} + 1\frac{1}{2} = 3\frac{5}{6}$

Fractions of Amounts

To find the fraction of an amount, all you need to do is divide the whole number by the denominator (Step 1), then multiply the answer by the numerator (Step 2)!

This is where the saying, 'divide by the bottom, times by the top' is used.

Example : $\frac{4}{7}$ of 35 = ?

Step 1 35 ÷ 7 = 5

↑ the denominator

1	2	3	4	5	6	7
5	5	5	5	5	5	5

= 35

35 is split into 7 equal parts. Each part is worth 5.

Step 2 5 × 4 = 20

↑ the numerator

1	2	3	4	5	6	7
5	5	5	5	5	5	5

= 35

We're finding the value of 4 parts here. 5 × 4 = 20.

$\frac{4}{7}$ of 35 = 20

Comparing & Ordering Decimals

Step 1
Write out the numbers you need to compare.

Example: 7.6   7.15   7.23   7.2   7.08

Step 2
Add zeros to the numbers to ensure each number is given to
the same number of decimal places, e.g. one, two or three.

Example: 7.6<u>0</u>   7.15   7.23   7.2<u>0</u>   7.08

Step 3
Compare each of the first digits from the left to see which
is larger, and order them from smallest to largest.

Example: <u>7</u>.60   <u>7</u>.15   <u>7</u>.23   <u>7</u>.20   <u>7</u>.08
Here they're all equal — 7 — so you don't need to re-order.

Step 4
Then move to the next column to the right to see which is
larger, and order them from smallest to largest.
Repeat as needed.

Example: 7.<u>6</u>0   7.<u>1</u>5   7.<u>2</u>3   7.<u>2</u>0   7.<u>0</u>8
             7.<u>0</u>8   7.<u>1</u>5   7.<u>2</u>3   7.<u>2</u>0   7.<u>6</u>0
Answer: 7.08   7.15   7.20   7.23   7.60

Comparing Fractions & Decimals

To compare a decimal and a fraction, you need to convert (change) them so they're either all decimals or all fractions.

To convert a fraction to a decimal, divide the numerator by the denominator. $\frac{1}{4} = 1 \div 4 = 0.25$

To convert a decimal to a fraction, multiply it by 100 and write it as the numerator. Write the denominator as 100. You can then simplify if needed. $0.25 = \frac{25}{100} = \frac{1}{4}$

Converting to decimals example

Order this list – $\frac{2}{8}$, 0.7, $\frac{2}{6}$, 0.36 – from lowest to highest.

Change fractions: $\frac{2}{8} = 0.25$. $\frac{2}{6} = 0.33$

As decimals it's: 0.25, 0.70, 0.33, 0.36

> Add zeros so each number is to the same decimal place.

From lowest to highest it's: 0.25, 0.33, 0.36, 0.70

The answer is: $\frac{2}{8}$, $\frac{2}{6}$, 0.36, 0.7

> In your answer, use the numbers from the original question.

Converting to fractions example

Order from lowest to highest: 0.25, $\frac{2}{4}$, $\frac{2}{5}$, 0.6, $\frac{2}{10}$

Convert the decimals. Change the fractions to be $\overline{100}$.

$0.25 = \frac{25}{100}$, $\frac{2}{4} = \frac{50}{100}$, $\frac{2}{5} = \frac{40}{100}$, $0.6 = \frac{60}{100}$, $\frac{2}{10} = \frac{20}{100}$

As fractions it's: $\frac{25}{100}$, $\frac{50}{100}$, $\frac{40}{100}$, $\frac{60}{100}$, $\frac{20}{100}$

From lowest to highest it's: $\frac{20}{100}$, $\frac{25}{100}$, $\frac{40}{100}$, $\frac{50}{100}$, $\frac{60}{100}$

So the answer is: $\frac{2}{10}$, 0.25, $\frac{2}{5}$, $\frac{2}{4}$, 0.6

FRACTIONS, DECIMALS & PERCENTAGES

MEASUREMENT

GEOMETRY

STATISTICS & MORE

Finding Percentages

Finding percentages is easy when you know how.
You can find 10% of a number by using place value.

To find 10%, you just need to divide the number by 10.
This means on a place value grid each digit becomes
10 times smaller, so moves one column to the right.
Example: What is 10% of 147? To find this, do 147 ÷ 10 = 14.7.

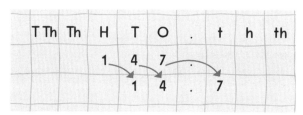

T Th	Th	H	T	O	.	t	h	th
		1	4	7	.			
			1	4	.	7		

10% of 147
= 14.7.

To find 1%, use exactly the
same method – just divide by
100 instead of by 10.
Example: What is 1% of 147?
To find this, do 147 ÷ 100 = 1.47.
1% of 147 = 1.47.

NINJA TIP:

If you don't know how many
places to move the digits,
look at the number of zeros
in 10 or 100.
10 has one zero, so move one
column to the right.
100 has two zeros, so move
two columns to the right.

To find 2%, you find 1%, then
multiply by 2.
Example: What is 2% of 147? To find this, do 147 ÷ 100 = 1.47
to find 1%. Then multiply 14.7 by 2, which is 29.4.
2% of 147 = 29.4.

Finding Percentages

Finding 5%

To find 5%, find 10%, then halve the amount.

Example: What is 5% of 120?

10% of 120 = 120 ÷ 10 = 12

half of 12 = 6, so 5% of 120 = 6

Finding percentages which are multiples of 10

To find a percentage that is a multiple of 10, e.g. 40%, 60% or 70%, first find 10% of the number. Then multiply this answer by the number of tens in the percentage. Example: there are 4 tens in 40%, so multiply the 10% answer by 4 to find 40%.

What is 20% of 470?

First find 10% of 470.

470 ÷ 10 = 47

2 × 47 = 94 (calculation below)

20% of 470 = 94

```
        4 7
  ×       2
  ─────────
        9 4
        1
```

What is 80% of 320?

First find 10% of 320.

320 ÷ 10 = 32

8 × 32 = 256

80% of 320 = 256

```
        3 2
  ×       8
  ─────────
      2 5 6
      2 1
```

Finding Percentages

First, remember the percentages you can easily find, such as 10%, 5%, 1% and 2%. You can use these percentages to find any other percentage by multiplying and adding.

Example: What is 46% of 230?
To find this, you can break it down into finding 40%, 5% and 1%, then add the totals together.

NINJA TIP:
With each step, make sure you note down the answers as you go, because you'll need them in later steps.

Step 1 Calculate 10%, then multiply this value by 4 to get 40%.
10% of 230 = 230 ÷ 10 = 23
23 x 4 = 92

```
    2  3
x      4
   ─────
    9  2
   ─────
    1
```

Step 2 Find 5% by halving the answer for 10%.
10% of 230 = 23.   23 ÷ 2 = 11.5   5% = 11.5

Step 3 Find 1% by dividing 10% by 10.
10% of 230 = 23.   23 ÷ 10 = 2.3   1% = 2.3

Step 4 Add the values of 5% and 1% together to get 6%.
11.5 + 2.3 = 13.8

Step 5 Add the value of 40% and 6% together to get 46%.
92 + 13.8 = 105.8

Finding Percentages: Long Multiplication

Finding percentages using other percentages (page 76) can be challenging, mostly because of the number of steps involved. The strategy described below involves only two steps. It's useful when finding tricky percentages like 83% or 67%.

Step 1 Carry out a long multiplication (see page 48).
Example: What is 46% of 230?

```
      2 3 0
  x     4 6
  _____
    1 3 8 0
    9 2 0 0
  _____
  1 0 5 8 0
```

NINJA TIP:
Remember to put in the place-holding zero. Try to put it in at the start when writing out the question. Then you won't forget it.

Step 2 Divide the answer by 100.

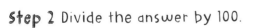

```
  1 0 5 8 0
  _____
    1 0 5 . 8 0
```

46% of 230 = 105.80

Measurement: Key Facts

Length

millimetre (mm) = one thousandth of a metre
centimetre (cm) = one hundredth of a metre
kilometre (km) = one thousand metres

10 millimetres (mm) = 1 centimetre (cm)
100 centimetres (cm) = 1 metre (m)
1000 metres (m) = 1 kilometre (km)

Weight

gram (g) = one thousandth of a kilogram
kilogram (kg) = one thousand grams
tonne (t) = one thousand kilograms

1 tonne (t) = 1,000 kilograms (kg)
1 kilogram (kg) = 1,000 grams (g)

Volume

millilitre (ml) = one thousandths of a litre
litre (l) – one thousand millilitres
kilolitre (kl) = one thousand litres

1 kilolitre (kl) = 1,000 litres (l)
1 litre (l) = 1,000 millilitres (ml)

Money: Coins & Notes

British Money

1p

2p

5p

10p

£5.00

£10.00

20p   50p   £1   £2

£20.00

£50.00

Change is what you receive if there is a difference between the cost of what you are buying and the money you hand over in cash. To calculate the change given, just subtract the cost from the money being used to pay.

Converting pounds to pence:

There are 100p in £1 so £1 is equal to 100p. Focus on converting the pounds first, then on any pence given after the decimal place.

Example: when converting £9.47, focus on the £9 which is equal to 900p, then on the remaining 47p. So, you have 947p.

NINJA TIP:

When working with money, you may have one figure in pence and another in pounds. Convert your pounds to pence to make it easier to calculate your answers. Example: What is £1.56 + 79p? Convert £1.56 to 156p. Now you can do 156 + 79 = 235p. Then convert back to pounds if you need to — £2.35.

Time:
Key Facts

Time vocabulary
millisecond
second
minute
hour
day
week
fortnight
month
year
decade
century
millennium

Days of the week
Monday
Tuesday
Wednesday
Thursday
Friday
Saturday
Sunday

Time
1,000 years = millennium
100 years = century
10 years = decade
1 year = 12 months
1 year = 52 weeks
1 year = 365 days
1 fortnight = 14 days
1 fortnight = 2 weeks
1 week = 7 days
1 day = 24 hours
1 hour = 60 minutes
1 minute = 60 seconds
half a minute = 30 seconds

Months of the year –
and how many days they last
January (31 days)
February (28 days/29 in a leap year)
March (31 days)
April (30 days)
May (31 days)
June (30 days)
July (31 days)
August (31 days)
September (30 days)
October (31 days)
November (30 days)
December (31 days)

Telling the Time

Identify the hands on the clock. The hour hand is shortest. The minute hand is longer. Some clocks have a seconds hand – this is long and thin and you can see it moving.

The numbers (and longest lines) refer to hours. All the lines refer to minutes and seconds.

O'clock The time is o'clock if the minute hand points to 12 – zero minutes have passed in the hour. The hour hand points straight at the hour number. The 24 hours in a day are split into two lots of 12 hours.

Half past The time is half past if the minute hand points to 6 – thirty minutes have passed. The minute hand is halfway around the clock.

After the minute hand passes half past the hour, we start to say 'to' instead of 'past' because the time is now closer to the next hour.

Quarter past / to 15 minutes is one quarter of 60, so 'quarter past' means 15 minutes past the hour (minute hand points to 3) and 'quarter to' means 15 minutes to the next hour (minute hand points to 9).

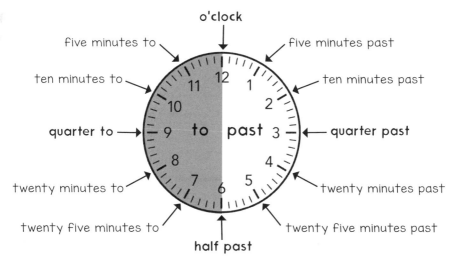

o'clock

five minutes to   five minutes past

ten minutes to   ten minutes past

quarter to → to past ← quarter past

twenty minutes to   twenty minutes past

twenty five minutes to   twenty five minutes past

half past

Telling the Time

There are 24 hours in a day, but the day is often split into two halves. We put 'am' after the first 12 hours of the day – midnight to midday. We put 'pm' for the next 12 hours. A 12-hour clock starts again at midday, so 1 o'clock in the morning or in the afternoon shows as 1 (1am or 1pm). A 24-hour clock carries on counting from 12 midday, so 1 o'clock in the afternoon is 13.

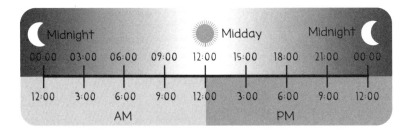

Analogue clocks use hands to point at lines and numbers on a clock face. **Digital clocks** use numbers only, like on phones or computers. Digital clocks often use the 24-hour system.

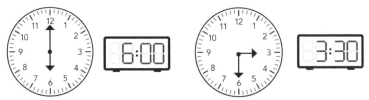

NINJA TIP:

If you multiply the hour number by five on an analogue clock, you will get the number of minutes.

Using a Ruler to Measure

Rulers are used to measure distances or lengths in millimetres (mm) and centimetres (cm). There are 10 mm in 1 cm. Rulers are very useful, but it is important to use them properly.

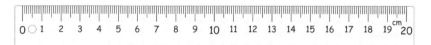

Centimetres are shown on the ruler with numbers and a longer line extending down. There are 10 mm (millimetres) for each cm, shown with much shorter lines. Half way between each cm point, there is a slightly longer line. This indicates half way between each cm, so 5 mm.

In order to measure accurately with a ruler, it is very important that you align the 0 point on the ruler with one end of what you need to measure.

Length: Conversion

It's important to be able to convert between units of length. All we need to do is think about place value and how we multiply and divide by 10, 100 and 1,000. It's that easy!

Conversion	What to do	Example
kilometres (km) to metres (m)	x 1,000	6 km x 1,000 = 6,000 m
metres (m) to kilometres (km)	÷ 1,000	5,000 m ÷ 1,000 = 5 km
metres (m) to centimetres (cm)	x 100	15 m x 100 = 1,500 cm
centimetres (cm) to metres (m)	÷ 100	670 cm ÷ 100 = 6.7 m
metres (m) to millimetres (mm)	x 1,000	9 m x 1,000 = 9,000 mm
millimetres (mm) to metres (m)	÷ 1,000	1,400 mm ÷ 1,000 = 1.4 m
centimetres (cm) to millimetres (cm)	x 10	17 cm x 10 = 170 mm
millimetres (mm) to centimetres (cm)	÷ 10	420 mm ÷ 10 = 42 cm

NINJA TIP:

Remember: maths questions on length will often give one number in kilometres (km) and the other in metres (m). Always try to convert so you are working with the same unit of measure for both numbers.

84

Mass: Measurement

Kilograms (kg) and grams (g) are used to measure the mass of something and can often be referred to as 'how much something weighs' or 'its weight'. Remember 1,000 grams = 1 kilogram.

Some scales only weigh amounts in grams. The scale shows chunks such as 50, 100, 150, and so on. It is important to work out what the smaller units in between are worth. If you look at 0–50 and try counting in 10s, you can see that each smaller unit is worth 10 grams.

g = grams

Other scales show kilograms, with ten smaller units in between each kilogram. As there are 1,000 grams in a kilogram, each of these shorter lines represent 100 grams.

kg = kilograms

NINJA TIP:

The measure shown on scales can be different. So, it is important to work out what the units in between are worth. This will help you take accurate measurements.

Mass: Conversion

It's important to be able to convert between units of mass. All we need to do is think about place value and how we multiply and divide by 10, 100 and 1,000. It's that easy!

Convert kilograms (kg) to grams (g) – multiply by 1,000
For example, 6 kg x 1,000 = 6,000 g.

Convert grams (g) to kilograms (kg) – divide by 1,000
For example, 5,000 g ÷ 1,000 = 5 kg.

NINJA TIP:

Remember: maths questions on mass will often give one number in kilograms (kg) and the other in grams (g). Always try to convert so you are working with the same unit of measure.

Example: What's 4.3 kg subtract 670 g?
Convert the 4.3 kg to grams – 4.3 kg x 1,000 = 4,300 g.
Now it is very simple to do 4,300 g subtract 670 g.

Volume & Capacity: Measurement

Volume is the amount of space taken up by an object. Capacity is the measure of an object's ability to hold a substance, such as a solid, a liquid or a gas.

Volume and capacity are measured in litres (l), millilitres (ml) and sometimes in centilitres (cl).

Ninja Maths Fact

Measuring cylinders or beakers are commonly used to measure how much of a liquid we have.

graduated cylinder

beaker

1 litre = 1,000 ml. The scales of beakers and measuring cylinders vary – they might increase in steps of 50 ml, 100 ml, 150 ml and so on. Remember to work out the value of the smaller units in between.

Volume & Capacity: Conversion

It's important to be able to convert between units of volume or capacity. All we need to do is think about place value and how we multiply and divide by 10, 100 and 1,000. It's that easy!

Convert litres (l) to millilitres (ml) – multiply by 1,000
For example, 4 l x 1,000 = 4,000 ml.

Convert millilitres (ml) to litres (l) – divide by 1,000
For example, 9,000 ml ÷ 1,000 = 9 l

NINJA TIP:

Maths questions on volume will often give one number in litres (l) and the other in millilitres (ml). Always try to convert so you are working with the same unit of measure.

Example: What is 8.2 l subtract 560 ml?
Convert 8.2 l to ml – 8.2 x 1,000 = 8,200 ml.
Now it is very simple to do 8,200 ml subtract 560 ml.

6 Geometry

2D Shapes

2D means two-dimensional. 2D shapes are flat.
2D shapes have two dimensions: length and width.

Some 2D shapes are *regular*, which means all the sides are the same length and all the internal angles are equal.

Some 2D shapes are *irregular*, which means the sides are different lengths and the internal angles are different.

Polygons are flat, two-dimensional shapes with straight sides that all join up. Here are some examples.

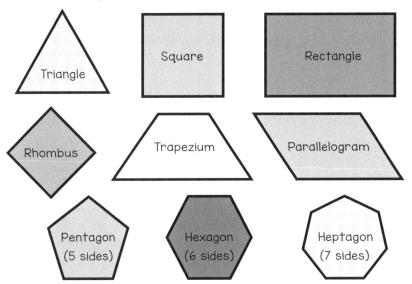

3D Shapes

3D means three-dimensional.

3D shapes have three dimensions — length, width and depth.

3D shapes have vertices, faces and edges.

A **vertex** is a corner. The plural (more than one) is vertices.

A **face** is a single flat surface.

An **edge** is a line between faces.

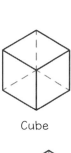

Cube

Cuboid

Sphere

Square-based
pyramid

Triangular
prism

Hexagonal
prism

Tetrahedron
(triangle-based
pyramid)

Cone

Cylinder

10   20   30   40   50   60

Calculating Perimeter

The perimeter is the distance around the sides of a 2D shape. In order to calculate the perimeter, we just need to add up the length of each side.

10 cm
2 cm   2 cm
10 cm

2 cm + 2 cm + 10 cm
+ 10 cm = 24 cm.
Perimeter = 24 cm.

More complex questions will require you to calculate the perimeter of compound or composite shapes (page 94). Calculating the perimeter of these shapes is also done by just adding up the lengths of all of the sides.

9 m + 8 m + 3 m + 3 m + 5 m +
4 m = 32 m. Perimeter = 32 m.

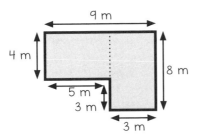

9 m
4 m
8 m
5 m
3 m
3 m

NINJA TIP:

Regardless of the type of shape you encounter, perimeter is just totalling the value of the length of each side.

Perimeter: Missing Values

Calculating the perimeter is harder when some lengths of the sides are missing. To find the value of the missing sides, you need to look at the lengths given on the shape.

Step 1 Look at which lengths are missing and which are given.

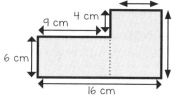

Step 2 Start with the horizontal lengths.

The longest horizontal length is 16 cm. That means whatever you add to 9 cm must equal 16 cm. 16 cm = 9 cm + ?. The missing length must be 7 cm.

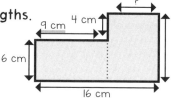

Step 3 Now look at the vertical sides.

The length of the longest side is still missing. You can work this out by adding 6 cm and 4 cm together. 6 cm + 4 cm = 10 cm.

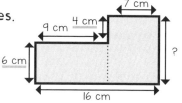

Step 4 Now add all the lengths together.

The perimeter of this shape is: 7 cm + 10 cm + 16 cm + 6 cm + 9 cm + 4 cm = 52 cm.

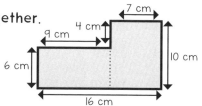

NINJA TIP:

Unless the question says to use a ruler, you need to use the lengths of the other sides to calculate the missing values, not a ruler - the lengths might not be accurate or to scale.

Area of a Rectangle / Parallelogram

Area is the amount of space inside the perimeter of a 2D shape. To calculate the area of a rectangle or parallelogram, you just need to follow simple formulas.

Ninja Maths Fact
length (l) x height (h)
= area of a rectangle
or parallelogram

Rectangle example
length 5 cm x height 10 cm = area 50 cm^2

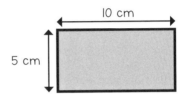

To calculate the area of a parallelogram you must multiply the width / base by the height of the parallelogram.

Parallelogram example
8 m x 3 m = 24 m^2

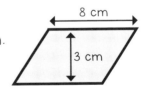

Ninja Maths Fact
Area is measured
in cm^2, m^2 or km^2.

NINJA TIP:

Maths questions with area are often not to scale - they might say a side is 10 cm but that's just a label, it's not really 10 cm. So don't use a ruler for these questions.

Area of a Compound Shape

A compound, or composite, shape is a shape made up of different shapes. To work out the area of a compound shape, you split it into smaller parts.

Step 1

To work out the area of this shape split it into two rectangles. Label them shape A and B.

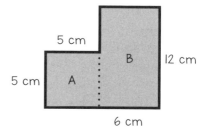

5 cm

B   12 cm

5 cm   A

6 cm

Step 2

Use the formula length x width to find the area of each rectangle.

Rectangle A – length 5 cm x width 5 cm = area 25 cm²

Rectangle B – length 12 cm x width 6 cm = area 72 cm²

Step 3

Add the two areas together to get the total area.

Area of rectangle A 25 cm² + area of rectangle B 72 cm² = total area 97 cm²

NINJA TIP:

Some shapes may need to be split into 3 or even 4 smaller rectangles to calculate the area. The same strategy applies – work out the area of each smaller rectangle, then add the area of each rectangle together.

Area of a Triangle

To calculate the area of a triangle you must multiply the width / base by the perpendicular (at a right angle/90°) height of the triangle, and then halve the total. It's like calculating the area of a rectangle, then halving it.

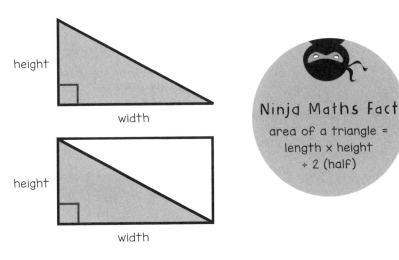

height

width

height

width

Ninja Maths Fact

area of a triangle =
length x height
÷ 2 (half)

Example 1
8 cm x 4 cm = 32 cm²
32 ÷ 2 = 16 cm²

Example 2
6 cm x 10 cm = 60 cm²
60 ÷ 2 = 30 cm²

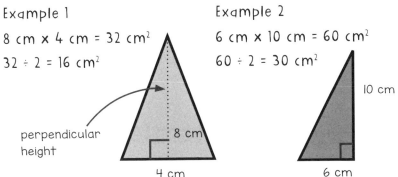

perpendicular
height

8 cm

4 cm

10 cm

6 cm

Volume of a Cuboid

The volume of a 3D cuboid is a measurement of the space that the shape takes up or occupies. Volume is measured in (unit)³ 'cubed', e.g. 36 m³, 2.6 cm³, 57 cm³.

Ninja Maths Fact

To calculate the volume of a cuboid just follow this simple formula:

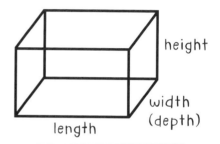

height

width (depth)

length

length x width x height = volume of a cuboid

Example 1
12 cm x 5 cm x 4 cm = 240 cm³

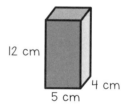

12 cm

4 cm

5 cm

Example 2
8 cm x 3 cm x 2 cm = 48 cm³

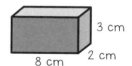

3 cm

2 cm

8 cm

NINJA TIP:
You can calculate volume in any order.
L x W x H, W x L x H, H x L x W, whichever way, you will get the same answer.

Angles: Right & Acute

A **right angle** is an angle exactly equal to 90 degrees. We can see many examples of right angles in daily life, such as the corner of a table or the corner of this book.

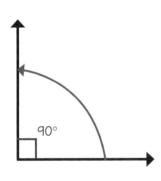

90°

Right angles are often shown by a small square in the corner of a shape. If you see this, the angle is 90 degrees.

Squares and rectangles contain four right angles.

An **acute angle** measures less than 90 degrees.

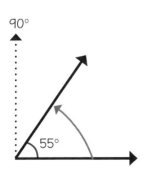

90°

55°

An easy way to remember what an acute angle is, is to think about it being a 'cute' angle - cute and small.

0.4

Angles: Obtuse, Straight Line, Reflex & Full Turn

An **obtuse angle** is an angle that measures more than 90 degrees and less than 180 degrees.

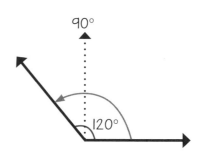

A **straight angle** is an angle equal to 180 degrees.

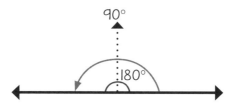

A **reflex angle** is a larger angle, it's always more than 180° (half a circle) but less than 360° (a full circle).

Angles: Using a Protractor

A **protractor** measures angles.

Step 1 Make sure the centre point of the protractor is on the vertex (the point where the two lines join the angle).

Step 2 Keep the centre point on the vertex and line up one of the zero lines on the protractor with one side of the angle.

Step 3 Read from the zero line along to the other side of the angle.

Step 4 Read the protractor carefully to get an accurate reading.

NINJA TIP:

Try rotating the angle that you are measuring on a piece of paper so that one of the sides is horizontal in front of you.

NINJA TIP:

If an angle's sides are short and difficult to measure, use a ruler to extend the side beyond the edge of the protractor.

Types of Triangles

An **equilateral triangle** is a triangle that has sides of equal length and three interior angles that are equal. The three angles inside an equilateral triangle will always be 60° as they must total 180°.

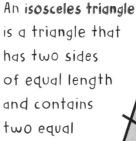

These lines show the sides are equal.

A **right-angled** triangle is a triangle which has one angle equal to 90 degrees – a right angle.

An **isosceles triangle** is a triangle that has two sides of equal length and contains two equal angles.

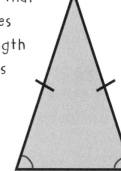

NINJA TIP:

The double lines on the sides of the triangle above tell us that these sides are equal in length.

Lines: Parallel, Perpendicular & Intersecting

Parallel lines are lines that are the same distance away from each other for their entire length.

Perpendicular lines are lines that meet at a right angle — 90°.

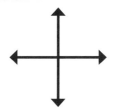

Intersecting lines are lines that cross over each other. The point at which the lines cross is called the 'point of intersection'.

NINJA TIP:

Calculating angles around intersecting lines is simple if you remember that there is 360° around the point of intersection. Straight line (180°) angles can easily be calculated by subtracting known angles from 180. See page 102.

Calculating Missing Angles

If you use what you know about the properties of shapes and angles, then finding missing angles becomes quite easy.

Missing angles in a triangle:

First, remember a triangle contains 180°. Subtract the two angles you know from 180 to find the missing angle.

Example: 52 + 68 = 120
180 - 120 = 60
d = 60°

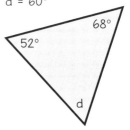

NINJA TIP:
Missing angles are easy to calculate in isosceles triangles because you know that two angles are equal.

Missing angles in a full turn:

First, remember that a full turn has 360°.
Add the angles you know together and then subtract from 360 to find the missing angle.

Example: 130 + 90 = 220
360 - 220 = 140
x = 140°

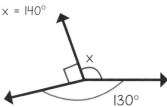

NINJA TIP:
Try to spot other symbols that indicate a specific angle, such as the small square for a right angle (90°).

Missing angles in a straight line:

First, remember that a straight line has 180°. Subtract the known angle from 180 to find the missing angle.

Example: 180 - 142 = 38
x = 38°

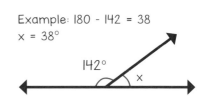

Mirror Lines

When something is symmetrical, it has two matching halves. You can check for symmetry in a shape by drawing a mirror line down the middle and seeing if both halves are identical. Symmetry can be seen around us in the real world.

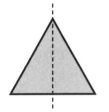 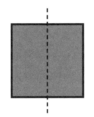 

In symmetry, the dashed line down the centre usually represents a mirror and how the image could be reflected to be symmetrical.

Reflection is when you change a shape's position as if it is reflected in a mirror. The shape itself does not change. First identify the corners of the shape you are reflecting.

One corner at a time, count from the mirror line to each corner. Then count from the mirror line the same amount on the reflection side and mark the reflected position. Then join your corners.

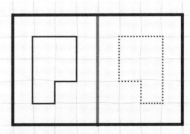

Circles: Diameter, Radius & Circumference

The radius is the distance from the centre of a circle outwards. You can calculate the radius if you know the diameter, you just need to halve the diameter.

The diameter goes straight across the circle, through the centre. You can calculate the diameter if you know the radius. You just need to double the radius.

The circumference is the distance once around the circle.

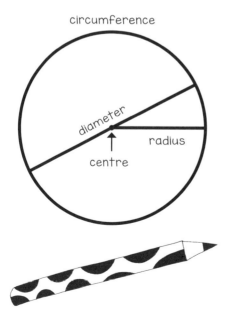

circumference

diameter

radius

centre

NINJA TIP:

Maths questions often use circles in pie charts and in angle questions. Try to remember that a circle is essentially a full-turn and contains 360°.

Turns & Rotation

When thinking about turns, remember your knowledge of fractions, halves and quarters as well as the angles 360°, 180° and 90°.

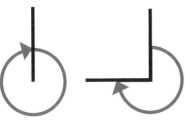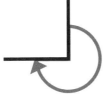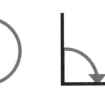

1 turn
is 360°.

$\frac{3}{4}$ turn
is 270°.

$\frac{1}{2}$ turn
is 180°.

$\frac{1}{4}$ turn
is 90°.

Clockwise means turning in the direction that a clock hand turns as it ticks.

Anti-clockwise means turning in the opposite direction that a clock hand turns as it ticks.

Coordinates

A graph has two axes, called the x axis and the y axis.
The **x axis** goes from left to right – it's horizontal.
The **y axis** goes from bottom to top – it's vertical.

Coordinates record where a point is on a graph, using numbers in brackets (x, y), e.g. (1,3). They are used to plot or place a point on the graph. The first number, the x number, is for the x axis and the horizontal position. The second number, the y number, is for the vertical position.

To plot coordinates, we first count horizontally along the x axis from the zero, then from that position we count vertically following the numbers on the y axis.

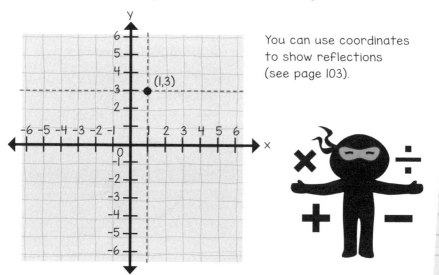

You can use coordinates to show reflections (see page 103).

Statistics & More

Charts & Graphs

Charts and graphs are used to represent data.

Pictograms use a picture to represent a number.

In the example, each image of a circle is equal to 6.
So you count in sixes.
A half circle is equal to 3, because 3 is half of 6.

Key ● = 6 points

Sports team	Number of points
Reds	●●◖
Blues	●●●
Yellows	●●●◖

Yellows have 6 + 6 + 6 + 3 = 21 points.

Tally charts are a simple way of noting numbers using lines. Tallying is done in fives, with groups of four vertical lines and a fifth line drawn diagonally across the four. One line means one unit of value.

Animal	Tally	Number
Worm	卌 卌 II	12
Ant	卌 卌 卌 卌 卌 II	27
Slug	III	3

Charts & Graphs

Pie charts show data using circles split into parts (segments).

The circle represents a total. The size of each segment shows how much of this total the segment represents.

Favourite Activities

☐ sleeping ■ eating
■ reading ☐ playing

Total number of people: 24

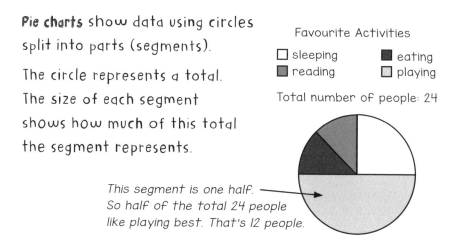

This segment is one half.
So half of the total 24 people like playing best. That's 12 people.

Bar graphs show data using vertical blocks or bars.

The labels tell you what the graph is showing.
The top of each bar lines up with a number on the y axis.
The number shows you how many the bar represents.

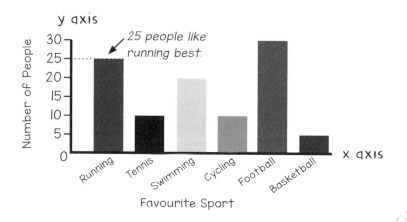

25 people like running best.

y axis

Number of People

x axis

Favourite Sport

Averages: Mean, Mode, Median, Range

You might be asked to calculate an average for a set of numbers. Averages can be represented in four different ways: the **mean, mode, median** and **range**.

Example set of numbers: 1, 3, 3, 5, 6, 7, 10

Mean To calculate the mean, add up all the numbers in the data set, then divide by the amount of numbers in the set.

1 + 3 + 3 + 5 + 6 + 7 + 10 = 35   35 ÷ 7 = 5   Mean = 5.

Mode The mode is the number that occurs the most or is the most frequent within the data set.

1, **3, 3**, 5, 6, 7, 10
3 occurs twice, the other numbers occur once. Mode = 3.

Median The median is the middle number in a list ordered lowest to highest or highest to lowest.

1, 3, 3, **5**, 6, 7, 10   Median = 5.

Range The range is the distance between the lowest and the highest number in the data set.

1, 3, 3, 5, 6, 7, 10   Lowest = 1 and highest = 10.   10 − 1 = 9.
Range = 9.

STATISTICS & MORE

Ratio & Proportion

Ratio is how much of one thing there is in relation to another thing.

Example: 'For every 30 pupils, we have 1 teacher'.

Proportion is how much there is of something compared to the total.

Example: 'Out of a group of 5 ninjas, there is 1 smaller ninja'.

Ratio and proportion are often used in recipes.
They are linked to fractions, percentages and measuring.

Ratio example: You want to make some blackcurrant squash.
You need 1 part squash to 6 parts water.
This means the ratio of squash to water is 1 : 6.

Proportion example: A cake has 8 slices. If one person eats 2 slices, what proportion of the cake have they eaten?
You can use fractions.
They have eaten $\frac{2}{8}$ slices, or $\frac{1}{4}$.
You could use percentages to show this as well. They have eaten 25%.

Algebra

Algebra refers to using a letter to represent a missing value we are trying to find.

This is useful when we're trying to find missing angles or lengths of shapes. It's also useful for missing values in pie charts and other data.

Example: $4 + ? = 12$
We can replace ? with a letter, such as x.
$4 + x = 12$

We can then rearrange this so we have the known numbers on one side of the equals sign and the unknown x on the other side.
$4 + x = 12$
$x = 12 - 4$
$x = 8$

Glossary

2D / two-dimensional: has two dimensions: length & width.

3D / three-dimensional: has three dimensions: length, width & depth.

Addend: a number added to another number.

Area: the amount of space inside a 2D shape.

Capacity: the maximum amount an object can hold.

Communicative: when you can reorder the parts in a sum & the answer is the same (works for + and x).

Composite number: has more than two factors.

Compound / composite shape: a shape made up of two or more shapes.

Cube number: a number multiplied by itself twice.

Denominator: the bottom number in a fraction; tells us how many equal parts the whole is made up of.

Difference: the answer when a number is subtracted from another.

Digit: number from 0–9.

Dividend: a number being divided by another number.

Divisor: a number dividing another number.

Equivalent fractions: are equal in value, with different numerators & denominators.

Factor: a number that divides into another without a remainder.

Fraction: represents parts of a whole.

Improper fraction: has a numerator bigger than the denominator.

Integer: a whole number.

Irregular shape: sides & angles are different sizes.

Minuend: a number we subtract another from.

Mixed number: a whole number and a fraction.

Multiple: what you get when you multiply a number by an integer.

Number bonds: pairs of numbers that add up to another number.

Numerator: the top number in a fraction; tells us how many equal parts of the whole there are.

Operation: an action like add, multiply or divide. The **operator:** is a symbol showing this, e.g. + or x.

Partition: split a number into smaller parts.

Perimeter: the distance around the sides of a 2D shape.

Place value: the value of a digit shown by its place or position in a number.

Prime number: is only divisible by 1 and itself.

Product: the total of two or more numbers multiplied together.

Proper fraction: has a numerator smaller than the denominator.

Quotient: the answer when a number is divided by another number.

Regular shape: sides & angles are equal sizes.

Remainder: an amount left over after a number has been divided.

Square number: the total of a number multiplied by itself.

Subtrahend: a number subtracted from another.

Sum: the total of two or more numbers added together.

Symmetry: when a shape has 2 matching halves.

Volume: the amount of space an object takes up.